WESTCHESTER PUBLIC LIB

P9-DNO-270

GREAT CAREERS IN THE SPORTS INDUSTRY™

DREAM JOBS IN SPORTS MEDIA

DANIEL E. HARMON

ROSEN
PUBLISHING®

New York

Published in 2015 by The Rosen Publishing Group, Inc.
29 East 21st Street, New York, NY 10010

Copyright © 2015 by The Rosen Publishing Group, Inc.

First Edition

All rights reserved. No part of this book may be reproduced
in any form without permission in writing from the publisher,
except by a reviewer.

Library of Congress Cataloging-in-Publication Data

Harmon, Daniel E.
Dream jobs in sports media/Daniel E. Harmon.
    pages cm. — (Great careers in the sports industry)
Includes bibliographical references and index.
ISBN 978-1-4777-7523-3 (library bound)
1. Mass media and sports—Vocational guidance. I. Title.
GV742.H37 2014
070.449796—dc23

                                                2013038830

Manufactured in the United States of America

CONTENTS

Radio talk-show host Mike Francesa (*left*) talks with former pro-football coach Dick Vermeil prior to the 2013 Super Bowl game.

Reporters like to repeat a well-known quip attributed to British author Douglas Adams: "I love deadlines. I like the whooshing sound they make as they fly by." The recurring stress of meeting deadlines, though, is no laughing matter.

Josh Katzowitz, a podcaster, freelance sportswriter, and former staff writer for daily newspapers, once blogged about a typical frenzy he weathered when covering a college basketball game. His deadline for the next day's newspaper was 10:45 PM. The game was expected to end around 10 o'clock. That should have given him ample time to conduct post-game player and coach interviews. He wrote most of his article on a laptop computer during the game, so he simply would need to insert the interviewees' comments and the final score.

Problems arose. The game lasted fifteen minutes longer than anticipated. Katzowitz had to alter his article draft because the team he assumed would lose (it was trailing by double digits late in the second half) made a last-minute comeback. It was 10:30 when he caught up with the coach after the game for a few quick questions while striding through the corridors. Then, while the coach conducted a press briefing, Katzowitz rushed to the locker room to interview a player. He literally ran back to the pressroom, inserted the quotations, finalized the story, and uploaded the file online to his newsroom.

Katzowitz rightly felt a sense of exhilaration at meeting the ultimate challenge of a sportswriter: "the deadline that I love and loathe."

ABC's *The Wide World of Sports* was a pioneering television series that covered a variety of sporting events from 1961 to 1998. Its famous introduction proclaimed its mission of showing viewers "the thrill of victory . . . and the agony of defeat." There is nothing like the emotions athletes feel in victory and defeat.

Broadcast audiences and print media readers get to experience those emotions indirectly. Sports coverage provides a similar rush for the media professionals who witness the action and make it real for their audiences. To do it effectively requires the ability to ignore pressure and work as a team.

Sports media and the way they operate have changed dramatically. In the 1800s, sometimes days or weeks elapsed before fans learned details of an event from their local newspapers. The invention of the telegraph and the laying of intercontinental cables greatly accelerated the speed of news transmission. Radio in the early 1900s began bringing listeners live coverage of major contests. Then came television, and today the Internet.

Sportswriters like Katzowitz and announcers like those who appeared weekly on *The Wide World of Sports* have exciting and satisfying careers. So do thousands of dedicated professionals who work away from the public eye. The U.S. Bureau of Labor Statistics (BLS) describes more than a dozen career fields involved in sports media. Print and broadcast employers need young workers talented and trained in writing and speaking, electronics and art, photography and personal communications. Just as teamwork is the key to athletic success, so it is to media efficiency.

Chapter I

THE PARTNERSHIP BETWEEN MEDIA AND ATHLETICS

Sports is big news worldwide. Athletic competition has been popular throughout history. What began in ancient times as personal contests attracted the notice of onlookers. Audiences gathered, and the proverbial "noise of the crowd" became part of athletics.

Even without the publicity of print and broadcast media and Internet news and entertainment sites, sports would continue. Fans would attend games. Thanks to modern media, though, sports doesn't merely continue. It is so popular that it has become engrained in the fiber of cultures on different continents. The great majority of enthusiasts who keep up with athletic competition aren't present at the scene; they enjoy the action from a distance.

Modern media have greatly expanded public interest in sports. They also have made it possible to increase coverage of minor sports and bring to public notice sports that formerly were little known. Media today cover sports at all levels: junior high and high school, college, professional, and amateur. Particularly notable has been

ESPN reporter Holly Rowe (*left*) interviews professional basketball star Candace Parker at a WNBA All-Star Game. Rowe began her career as a newspaper sportswriter.

the great increase in women's sports coverage in the past forty years.

Most exposure naturally goes to the most popular sports: baseball, soccer, football, hockey, basketball, tennis, auto racing, golf, boxing, and mixed martial arts. Summer and Winter Olympics occur only every four years, but when they do, they command prominent international headlines.

Minor sports include softball, wrestling, Canadian and arena football, bowling, volleyball, horse racing, rugby, lacrosse, gymnastics, track and field, weight lifting, and water sports. Once-obscure sports such as highland games (caber toss, sheaf toss, stone put) are becoming somewhat familiar. Media even cover new sports such as disk golf and bossaball.

Media coverage is important for sports programs to entertain and impact the public. On the flipside, sporting events provide valuable entertainment and news for the media. Sports has become big business, thanks primarily to the press. Broadcasting networks pay major sports leagues billions of dollars annually for the right to televise games. In recent years, the four major professional sports leagues have established their own networks: the NFL Network (National Football League), NBA TV (National Basketball Association), MLB Network (Major League Baseball), and NHL Network (National Hockey League).

The obvious dream jobs in sports media belong to the professionals who report and broadcast the action. Sports enthusiasts see their bylines and faces regularly. Some journalists earn celebrity status.

For every byline and face, many other media specialists are needed. Photographers and camera operators bring events to life visually. Editors ensure accurate and grammatically correct writing. Graphic designers put together attractive sports sections in magazines and newspapers. Unseen technicians see to it that broadcasts go on the air without a hitch. Marketing and public relations specialists keep athletes and sports organizations in the public mind during off-seasons and between games.

THRIVING ON PRESSURE

Reporters learn to conquer deadlines. Some actually love the pressure. In fact, some say writing under pressure is the only way they can produce good copy. To them, it's an incomparable adrenaline rush.

Dave Kindred, an author and award-winning sportswriter for major newspapers and magazines, once gave himself an interesting assignment: write an eight-hundred-word blog column in less than forty minutes. He titled it "A Deadline Column About Writing on Deadline." He started writing at 9:52 AM and allowed himself until 10:30 to complete it.

Kindred's column was about how various sportswriters and authors have gone about beating deadlines. He offered tips he learned from the masters; for example, do much of your drafting and editing (not just note taking) while the event is in progress, and don't wait until it's over to begin writing. Train yourself to tune out the noise of the stadium or coliseum and the hubbub inside the press box. Don't spend halftime relaxing in the press hospitality room. "Take the time to review your notes, get them in order; the more preparation you do during the event, the less you need to do later."

To Kindred, a deadline is a glorious challenge. "It's a test, it's a dare, it's a game within the game."

Kindred finished writing his column one minute early, with two words extra.

MEDIA PERSONALITIES

Understandably, the sports media professionals who immediately come to mind are those who are in the public eye and ear. Sports fans regularly follow the writings of newspaper and magazine reporters and columnists. Announcers and analysts for college and pro sports radio networks are familiar voices. Veteran television announcers and color commentators appear on game-day telecasts.

Although they are able to report the action without a misstep, these media personalities work under constant pressure. Play-by-play announcers, especially on TV, must state every detail accurately. A blunder will be observed plainly by millions in the audience.

LeBron James, winner of the NBA's Most Valuable Player Award, reads the newspaper sports pages in a hotel lobby. Sportswriters and announcers have dubbed the standout forward "King James."

Sports columnists for print media usually turn in their material well before press deadlines. Reporters covering night games, however, may have only minutes to finalize their stories and submit them to their editors electronically. In recent years, pressures have intensified. If a newspaper's management decides to guarantee home delivery by 5 AM, for example, the press deadline for reporters and editors must be moved up also. A typical sportswriting deadline for a daily paper is 10:45 the evening before. Some games have barely ended by that time. Some are still in progress. Highly touted games in later time zones may not have started yet. Those reports obviously can't make the next day's dawn edition; they will appear in a second edition distributed to news racks a few hours later.

Even for games that end long before a press deadline, reporters may be expected to file early accounts for online editions as soon as they can.

Veteran sports journalists become well acquainted with many of the athletes and coaches they cover over a period of years. They get to watch players flourish from bashful high school and college amateurs, working ardently to develop their talents, to famous stars basking in the spotlight. They follow coaches' careers and observe how each approaches the mission of getting the best from every player.

"HOW YOU PLAYED THE GAME"

Probably the most famous line in sports literature is from "Alumnus Football," a poem by Grantland Rice (1880–1954) published in 1908. It concludes:

"For when the One Great Scorer comes to mark against your name, He writes—not that you won or lost—but how you played the Game."

Many high-profile coaches and players, as well as their fans, scorn that noble philosophy today. They insist that in competition, winning is everything. Toward that end, cheating is acceptable as long as it goes unpenalized. Most sportswriters, though, still hold to the principle that competition should be fair and honest.

Grantland Rice was followed and admired nationally for his syndicated sports columns, radio broadcasts, and poems. His commentaries made legends of many athletes. It was Rice who cast the 1924 Notre Dame football backfield as nothing less than modern mythological heroes. His widely reprinted tribute, which appeared the day after the Fighting Irish defeated Army that year, began, "Outlined against a blue-gray October sky, the Four Horsemen rode again. . . ."

Rice played football and baseball at Vanderbilt University. After graduation in 1901, he had no clear career goal. He considered pro baseball but doubted he could last long because of a lingering arm injury. Although he acquired no journalism credentials in college, he brashly applied to a small start-up newspaper for the job of sports editor. The editor told him the paper had no sports department. If Rice would be willing to cover state government, court, and other news beats, he could write about sports on the side.

He took the job. The rest is sports journalism history.

INVISIBLE BUT ESSENTIAL MEMBERS OF A MEDIA TEAM

Sports audiences are familiar with the voices and faces of broadcasters and the bylines of writers. No less important are many unfamiliar professionals who put together print periodicals and broadcast programs.

Sports photographers usually get their names attached in small print to their published images, but many readers don't see them. Without the exciting visual impact they provide, however, the periodical would be dull indeed. Almost never mentioned except in the periodical's masthead are the editors who make writing and photo assignments and review and approve all the articles and images. The same is true of copy editors and proofreaders who scrutinize every word of every story for mistakes, and page designers who make the total print product look attractive.

In broadcast productions, behind-the-scenes personnel include program producers, directors, audio-video editors, camera operators, and broadcast and sound engineering technicians. Online sports media need various individuals with expertise in computer programs and digital communications technology.

PUBLICITY MAKERS

Professional, college, and some high school sports programs hire media specialists to build and maintain positive reputations for them. These professionals include marketing, public relations (PR), and advertising managers and the staff specialists they supervise. Copywriters, editors, art directors, and graphic designers work in these departments.

Marketing, PR, and ad firms produce publicity materials for all types of media: news releases and articles for print publications, commercials for TV and radio, and a combination of items for Web platforms.

DEMANDING WORK PAYS OFF

Like writers and broadcast reporters, all of the other media professionals frequently work under pressure. Photographers have the same (in some cases earlier) deadlines than reporters. Newspaper and magazine editors finalize each edition of a periodical—and they can't send it to press until the work of their writers and photographers has been approved and laid out on the pages. Broadcast producers,

A television director (*right*) and technician discuss a program at the mixing console inside a TV gallery. Broadcast teams also include producers, camera operators, and editors.

directors, editors, camera operators, and technicians together have to ensure that programs are produced satisfactorily and precisely on time. Marketing, public relations, and advertising professionals establish and follow firm schedules. They often work on two or more projects simultaneously, which means falling behind with one project's timetable can impact all their other work.

But perseverance pays. Actually, most lifelong sports media professionals ultimately have longer and more profitable careers than most professional athletes. Some pro athletes are paid six- and even seven-figure salaries.

However, their careers are usually over by the time they're in their late thirties. Media personnel generally work into their sixties and beyond. Most athletes peak in performance by age thirty. Writers, photographers, and broadcast professionals, on the other hand, improve steadily through the years; many are most productive and turn in their finest work late in life.

On the whole, sports media professionals enjoy much better job security than athletes, where competition for a slot on the roster is fierce and pressure to stay there is constant. Many standout athletes this year will be replaced next year by younger talent, even though the veterans are still good players. On media staffs, most professionals can expect to keep their jobs as long as they perform well.

SPORTS MEDIA ARE GAINING HEIGHTENED IMPORTANCE

In print and television newsrooms, sports journalists were once accustomed to a lower status than journalists who cover government, politics, breaking dramas, and other daily headline-generating matters. The sports staff jokingly has been dubbed the "toy department." Sports pages are relegated to the inside sections of newspapers. Sports reports come near the end of television news programs.

Sports always will be secondary news, by comparison, but sports media professionals receive the same

Sports became headline news when a U.S. House of Representatives committee in 2008 held a hearing on steroid use by Major League Baseball players.

respect today as their counterparts. Sports is no longer purely an entertainment medium; often, sports news is mainline news. Those in sports media careers must prepare just as diligently and work just as hard on the job as their colleagues in other departments. When it comes to action and visual effects, they're in prime positions to deliver what most excites reading and viewing audiences.

Chapter 2

BEGIN PURSUING YOUR INTERESTS NOW

Many young students assume there is nothing they can do for now to prepare for a career. High school graduation may be years away. Workplaces are changing at a dizzying pace, driven by advancing technology. Because of that, there seems little likelihood jobs will be performed the same way five years from now that they are today.

The reality is that it's never too early in life to think about a career. Despite changes in how jobs are done, basic job roles remain relatively unchanging. By their senior year in high school, students should be giving serious thought to a general career field. Your career interests while in high school probably will determine your post-graduation plan.

Even while in school, students can take steps that may give them an advantage when it's time to enter the workforce. Here are some things sports-minded young people can do if they are interested in media careers.

GO TO "WORK" FOR YOUR HIGH SCHOOL OR COLLEGE

Students with good writing skills and interests can get early experience writing for school newspapers and yearbooks. A few are appointed editors. A bit of school newspaper writing experience could lead to actual part-time employment while in school. Many local weekly newspapers and a few dailies pay talented students to function as stringers, reporting on their schools' sports. Student

Students in a high school journalism class learn how a variety of computer programs and other technology are useful to media professionals.

writers should also consider contributing to the publications of local volunteer organizations.

You can contribute articles, take photos, and perform computer and design tasks for school-related Web projects. If none exist, think about starting a blog or Web site devoted to your school's athletic program—with the administration's consent. While you're at it, contribute posts to established sports blogs. Posting to some of the feedback threads of sports articles published online can be excellent training for a budding sports writer. (Be a thoughtful poster. Submitting inflammatory, poorly constructed comments for the Internet sports community to see is not a good start in Internet writing.)

Avid young photographers can also gain experience on school newspaper staffs. They, too, may land night and weekend assignments covering events for local newspapers. At the same time, they can volunteer to assist local professional photographers. Assistants help carry equipment and may get to observe as their mentors edit images onscreen.

Advances in photo technology tend to work in favor of young people wanting to try their hand. The BLS notes "the decreasing cost of digital cameras and the increasing number of amateur photographers and hobbyists. Improvements in digital technology reduce barriers of entry into this profession and allow more individual consumers and businesses to produce, store, and access photographic images on their own."

Students are on the air at their high school radio station. This station in Burlington, Wisconsin, began broadcasting in 1975.

Students drawn by the excitement of broadcasting might find opportunities while still in their teens. Many colleges and some high schools operate student-run radio stations.

Teenagers today have become adept at developing videos to post on YouTube, blogs, and other social network outlets. Many of their efforts are very well planned, prepared, produced, and presented. A young sports enthusiast can establish an early reputation by committing time to present a careful diet of video-rich blog content, perhaps including school sports interviews.

ATHLETES WHO TURN TO JOURNALISM

All of the major sports television networks employ noted former athletes to provide color commentary when broadcasting events. Similarly, many sportscasters for local and regional radio productions were standout athletes in college.

Well known to followers of ESPN's *Monday Night Football* (*MNF*) is Lisa Salters. The veteran TV journalist roves the sidelines and enlivens each broadcast with coach and player interviews, injury updates, and insights as each game progresses.

While majoring in broadcast journalism at Pennsylvania State University, Salters played guard on the women's basketball team. (At 5 feet 2 inches ([1.6 meters]) tall, she was the team's shortest player ever.) After graduating in 1988, she became a general assignment reporter for a Baltimore television station, then was hired by ABC News. She covered major national and international events, including the trials of the Oklahoma City bombers in 1997 and the Winter Olympics in Japan in 1998.

Since joining ESPN in 2000, the award-winning journalist has covered sporting events and feature topics worldwide. She was host of the 2006 Winter Olympic coverage from Italy. She appeared as the sideline reporter for *Saturday Night Football* on ABC for five seasons before assuming the similar role for *MNF* in 2012. Salters is also a prominent correspondent on ESPN's television news magazine, *E:60*, and reports at National Basketball Association games.

Sports-minded students who possess artistic skills eventually may work for advertising, marketing, public relations, and design firms. They can get early experience with school publications.

Many high schools and some junior high schools teach basic courses in art and design. Graphic designers entering the job market need impressive portfolios. They can begin accumulating examples of their best work in high school and college. Art faculty will help them build effective portfolios and put them in contact with potential employers.

START A RÉSUMÉ

If you are old enough to mow lawns or babysit for spending money, you are old enough to create your résumé. Those early odd jobs appearing at the top of your employment file will impress prospective employers in the future.

Your résumé is your basic record about yourself, insofar as employers might be concerned. It tells your career ambition, personal interests, special skills, educational level and background, school classes and activities related to your vocational interest, and work experience. A résumé is a vibrant, living file. Each time you make a change, adding a new job credit or educational achievement, you will update it. Your résumé undoubtedly will expand and grow more impressive year by year until you retire.

A SAMPLE RÉSUMÉ

Maria Washington
192 Fourteenth Street
Swain, Nebraska 52000
Home: (003) 234-5678; Mobile: (003) 987-5678
mdwashington@sub50hh.com

Immediate Objective: To obtain a part-time or internship position with the sportscasting staff of a broadcast station or network.

Long-Term Objective: Sportscaster.

Education
Swift Creek High School (Swain, Nebraska), Class of 2015 (3.0 GPA).

Work Experience
2013–Present
Part-time sales clerk, McElveen Sporting Goods, Swain.

School Years 2013–2014 and 2014–2015
Sportswriter for the *Swift Creek Cork* student newspaper.

2014–Present
Writer, narrator, and producer of high school sports video features for the Swift Creek High student blog.

Special Skills and Knowledge
Experienced with Windows and Mac computers, Android smartphone and tablet devices, productivity software, mobile apps, and social networks. Recording, narrating, and editing audio for sports-related student blog projects.

Elective courses in public speaking and voice/diction.

School debate team, 2014–2015.

Three years of German language studies.

Activities
Emceeing school programs. Public address announcing at home basketball games.

Helping staff the phone banks for local radio fund-raising campaigns.

References
Madelyn Ewing, co-owner, McElveen Sporting Goods, Swain; phone (003) 254-2345.

Willard Ferguson, debate team coach, Swift Creek High School; phone (003) 254-4321.

This example of a résumé for a part-time or internship position in sportscasting highlights experience in sportswriting and sports video production.

If you have no work experience right now, you can start what human resources officers call a functional résumé. It focuses on your interests, talents, and skills. When you enter the workforce, this will evolve into a chronological résumé, presenting your employment history.

GO JOB HUNTING—EVEN IF YOU AREN'T READY TO WORK

Investigate the specific careers in which you are interested. Spend much time exploring Web sites of newspapers, magazines, television and radio stations, broadcast networks, sports e-magazines and newsletters, and sports blogs. Look for the staff directory to learn what positions an organization fills. Read the bios of staff members to learn their backgrounds.

Many entities post job openings online. Although you may not be qualified and are nowhere near the job search stage of your life, read the job descriptions. Note the required levels of education and experience. Create a job notebook for your future reference. Organize it into general job categories and subcategories. Cut and paste the job descriptions you find online into word processing files. Compare to see whether different employers have different requirements for what appear to be similar jobs.

From time to time, check the career category descriptions maintained by the BLS in its *Occupational Outlook*

Handbook (www.bls.gov/ooh). Job titles change, and information is revised periodically. Generally, though, the current descriptions are relevant and accurate.

For example, students interested in sportswriting careers will find this notation in the *OOH*: "Opportunities are expected to be limited because of both the number of workers who are interested inentering this field and declines in the number of positions. Prospects should be best for those with experience in the field, often gained through internships or by working on school papers."

Young people will find that most local professionals are more than willing to share information and advice. College and some high school internships with media organizations may be available in your area.

Chapter 3

EQUIPPING YOURSELF FOR A SPORTS MEDIA CAREER

For young people who are serious about a media career, a smart first step is volunteering to work for the school newspaper, a Web initiative, or a broadcasting project. Volunteering provides a taste of what the work is like in the business world. If these individuals do enter a sports media career, this early experience will have provided a basic foundation. It will also make valuable entries on their résumés.

CRUCIAL TRAITS OF MEDIA PROFESSIONALS

Successful media professionals possess certain natural personality traits. Some characteristics apply to almost all media jobs. Others relate to particular occupations.

PRINT MEDIA

News gatherers and commentators for print, TV/radio, and Internet media all need excellent writing and communication skills. They must be "people people," able to engage strangers and draw out interesting information and comments. A strong sense of social perception is needed—the ability to put themselves in the reader's place and consider how an idea or statement could be misinterpreted. They must possess stamina and perseverance, determined to get at the important facts when interviewees are evasive. Authors of books and lengthy article series must be diligent, patient researchers.

For interviewers, the ability to listen well is vital. It's wise for an interviewer to prepare a mental or written question set in advance. But rather than thinking ahead to the next question to ask, the reporter should pay close attention to what the person is saying from moment to moment. The best comments usually aren't drawn from planned questions. They come after putting aside the script and opening new lines of questioning when the interviewee makes interesting, unexpected remarks.

Editors oversee the work of writers and must be good writers themselves. They also must have good planning, management, and decision-making skills. They need to be detail-oriented. Modern editors are experienced in computer programs, including digital production systems.

Good photographers are creative and have an eye for interesting subjects, angles, and image composition. To a large degree, photography is an art form. Photographers should be interested in technology and should have mechanical skills. Good communication skills and business sense will be needed, especially if they become self-employed.

BROADCAST MEDIA

Students interested in announcing positions naturally must have excellent speaking voices. Clarity and delivery can be improved by voice instruction. In the past, physical attractiveness was a major consideration in getting jobs as television broadcasters and personalities. Physical discrimination is much less a factor now. Still, TV broadcasters must have a neat, professional appearance.

Broadcast reporters must have good people skills as well as research and writing abilities. As in practically all other media careers, they need to be proficient with computers.

Announcers and broadcast reporters must possess an extra measure of persistence. The BLS points out that competition for on-the-air jobs is intense, and applicants may have to audition at many stations before being hired.

Broadcasting producers and directors, like print editors, must have excellent leadership, management,

Basketball sportscaster and commentator Dan Dakich, shown here at the National Invitation Tournament, is a former college player and coach.

and communication skills. They should be inquisitive and eager to master all aspects of program production.

Video camera operators rely on much the same instincts and skills as print media photographers, though the equipment and techniques they use are quite different. They need good eye-hand coordination and vision. Most sports video shooting is done with digital equipment, and the camera operators' work is edited on computers. Operators and editors need to be familiar with a variety of video editing applications.

MARKETING AND PUBLIC RELATIONS

Young people thinking of marketing, advertising, or public relations careers in the sports realm must be good time managers and decision makers. They must have good analytical instincts, especially since emerging digital media have started new trends in advertising and marketing methods. Marketing and PR professionals have to interact well with countless individuals—coworkers as well as clients and others outside their organizations. They need to be receptive to creative ideas for developing promotional campaigns.

PR specialists need strong skills in research and writing. Most PR jobs involve public speaking. Professionals need to have good speaking voices; training in voice and diction may be beneficial.

Applicants for meeting- and event-planning jobs must have excellent organizational, communication, problem-solving, and negotiation skills. They have to stay composed under pressure. Fairly advanced computer knowledge is important because they will be making regular use of social media and virtual meeting platforms in their work. They will likely be using financial and data management software.

ART AND GRAPHIC DESIGN

Professionals in graphic design and art direction obviously need artistic and creative instincts. They need good

An artist uses a computerized tablet in his work. Art and design professionals today must be skilled with different types of software.

communication skills for interacting with clients and coworkers. Time-management discipline is critical. Art directors need good leadership qualities; designers must be good team workers.

Professionals in this field should be familiar with all traditional art forms, but most of the work today is computer-intensive. Although designers work with standard art supplies at drafting tables and light tables, they must also also be proficient with software for illustration, image editing, and file organization.

INTERNSHIP OPPORTUNITIES

Some young people obtain part-time jobs in sports media while in college or high school. This early experience becomes the basis for what they will accomplish in the future. Here, they start to determine their specific career interests. Those who decide to pursue work as print or broadcast reporters begin to develop their original "style."

They receive a valuable boost at this early stage if they can land an internship with a sports publisher or broadcast company. Internships are available with magazines and large daily newspapers, TV stations, and broadcast networks. Regardless of the pay (or non-pay), an internship can provide a foot in the door for an excellent first job.

TECHNOLOGY AND STATISTICS

Students interested in technology careers need other qualities besides computer and electronics wizardry and manual dexterity. They must be good problem solvers and must be eager to listen to and cooperate with coworkers. Technicians who go into business for themselves must be able to market their services and manage their businesses.

Students who take an interest in the technical side of sports media should be good in math and physics. Electronics courses are especially important.

Media statisticians, as the job title suggests, must be math-minded. They have high aptitudes for critical thinking and problem solving. Most jobs involve report writing and oral communication with team members.

EDUCATIONAL REQUIREMENTS

Different levels of education are required for different sports media jobs. They range from high school diplomas to master's degrees and doctorates. Most jobs require a bachelor's or associate's degree.

WRITERS, REPORTERS, AUTHORS, AND EDITORS

High school students interested in print journalism careers should consider college programs in journalism or other communications curricula that encompass journalism. They learn interviewing techniques and the fundamental who-what-when-where-how-why approach to terse news writing. Their curricula may require courses in subjects such as government, physical sciences, and a foreign language.

Some print writers have degrees in majors such as history, English, and political science. They hone their reportorial talents on the job, usually starting with small assignments.

Many veteran freelance writers and book authors have backgrounds in journalism. Others have English degrees.

Editors usually begin with the same training as reporters and rise from the ranks. They obtain undergraduate degrees in journalism or another branch of communications, or English. Many editors for large publications hold master's degrees.

Some colleges and universities offer graduate degrees in one or more branches of communications. Many grad students are individuals who obtained undergraduate degrees in other areas and then decided to enter the journalism profession.

ANNOUNCERS AND BROADCAST JOURNALISTS

Some of the successful announcers of the past never attended college. They began as youngsters hanging around local radio and TV stations. Keenly interested to learn about and take part in the miracle media of the airwaves, they offered to carry out the trash, run errands, bring in food for the staff and assist in any other way, just to get a foot inside the station. A few managed to persuade station owners to let them work as DJs, spinning records on late-night shifts. They went on the air as "announcers" for piddling or no pay. If they gathered a following of listeners, they were given daytime on-air slots. The most popular and persevering young announcers finally rose to well-paying shifts with larger stations.

Today, hanging around a studio as a teenager isn't a bad idea. However, students planning to pursue careers in radio and/or television broadcasting should consider college programs in broadcasting. Many colleges enfold broadcasting studies within journalism or mass communication majors.

Public address system announcers at sports events generally do not need a college degree. They learn during a brief period of on-the-job training from an experienced announcer.

PRODUCERS AND DIRECTORS

There are few formal training programs for producers and directors. Most who work on television and radio programs have college degrees in broadcasting or another communications curriculum. Some take courses and may earn degrees in business or management.

Typically, producers and directors begin their careers as broadcast reporters, announcers, or technical personnel.

PR, MARKETING, AND ADVERTISING PROFESSIONALS

Most public relations workers have bachelor's degrees in public relations or another branch of communications studies, such as journalism. Some business and English majors go into the PR field.

Entry-level PR workers often learn on the job, beginning by performing clerical chores. They might be assigned to clip press articles and build profile material for the organization. They later are assigned to research and write press releases and feature articles under the supervision of a manager or veteran staffer.

For public relations management roles, applicants may need as much as five to ten years of staff experience. Their educational background should include training in business and public affairs. According to recent statistics, a fourth of PR managers had master's degrees. The Public Relations Society of America (www.prsa.org) offers a certification program.

Advertising, marketing, and promotions managers need a bachelor's degree in advertising or a related program like journalism or PR. They will likely take courses in marketing and market research, sales, consumer behavior, communication methods, and new media technology. They may also need training in economics, business law, finance, accounting, and statistics.

Some meeting- and event-planning professionals earn their positions by proving themselves at running fast-tempo, high-pressure functions such as catering. Increasingly, planning applicants are expected to have a bachelor's degree as well as on-the-job experience. The ideal college major is hospitality management. Alternative study concentrations might be marketing, business, and public relations or another communication category. Certification, not required but helpful for advancement, is offered by the Convention Industry Council.

GRAPHIC DESIGNERS AND ART DIRECTORS

Most media artists hold degrees in art or graphic design. Courses typically include design principles, commercial graphics, computer-aided design, Web design, photography, illustration, fine art, and print techniques. Useful elective courses include marketing, writing, and business.

Some art directors come from early careers in related fields like fine art, photography, and writing/editing. They may acquire post-secondary degrees in majors such as business administration.

Graphic design internships are available for college students. Faculty serve as liaisons between graduating students and employers.

PHOTOGRAPHERS AND VIDEO CAMERA OPERATORS

College degrees are not required for most photography positions. However, young photographers should take courses to increase their knowledge of techniques and equipment. Training, experimentation, and practice are part of a lifelong learning process.

Students interested in photojournalism and newspaper staff careers may pursue journalism degrees. They learn various aspects of publishing in addition to photography. Courses in art and design are helpful. Business, accounting, and marketing courses will be useful for photographers who intend to go into business for themselves.

Many video camera operators also pursue journalism or related degrees in college. Some college programs include courses in video camera operation and editing.

STATISTICIANS

Some statisticians enter the career field with bachelor's degrees in mathematics or statistics. Most have master's degrees; some hold doctorates. Besides statistics, sample courses usually include calculus, probability theory, mathematical modeling, and computer science.

BROADCAST AND SOUND ENGINEERING TECHNICIANS

Some technicians begin in assistant roles with only a high school diploma or GED. They master the technology

A broadcast engineer for a media syndicate monitors Major League Baseball games as they are streamed to subscribers who use desktop computers and mobile devices.

on the job and advance with experience. Most, though, acquire associate's degrees or vocational certificates.

Formal training courses and programs usually last from a few months to a year. A central part of training is learning to use basic broadcast and sound engineering equipment. The best advancement opportunities are for technical professionals with associate's or bachelor's

degrees in areas such as electronics, computer networks, and broadcast technology. Most chief engineers at large stations have engineering degrees.

Certification is not required but improves advancement potential. The Society of Broadcast Engineers offers certification programs for various types of technical jobs.

Quickly advancing technology requires even veteran technicians to enroll frequently in workshops and continuing education classes.

Chapter 4

PUTTING ACTION ON PAPER

The best sportswriters are those who find fresh topics to write about, engage readers with intriguing leads, and provide information that readers find worthwhile as well as entertaining. A reserve guard in a basketball game hurls a winning three-pointer from mid-court at the buzzer. That epic effort becomes the focus of the story. Which team won and the numerical score might not even be mentioned until the fourth or fifth paragraph of the article.

Sports fans thrill to read such accounts. Young student writers imagine themselves filing such reports.

Sports journalism blossomed as a worthy and exciting profession in the early 1900s. Since then, action-minded writers have flocked to that branch of media careers. Sports media also provide rewarding careers for photographers and editors.

Periodicals at all levels cover sports. They include small weekly newspapers, dailies in cities of every size, and newspapers and magazines with national and international distributions. Popular magazines like *Sports*

Journalists for multiple organizations cover a World Cup soccer match. The Internet enables reporters to file their stories instantaneously from remote locations.

Illustrated, *Runner's World*, and *Baseball Digest* are devoted entirely to sports coverage. So are certain regional periodicals and magazines produced by college alumni and booster groups. Among the most sought-after jobs are those with syndication services, such as the Associated Press and Reuters.

SPORTSWRITERS, CORRESPONDENTS, AND AUTHORS

Print media journalists write for newspapers, magazines, and wire/online services. Reporters develop networks of insiders who regularly supply them with information and suggest ideas for articles. On game days and nights, they cover the action on-site.

Sports reporters and correspondents research and write stories assigned to them by their editors. Besides attending sports events, they interview athletes, coaches, and others to obtain information, opinions, and quotations. They search for additional information from other published sources, typically online.

Sportswriters and correspondents spend more time in the field, interviewing subjects and gathering news, than

C. C. Sabathia, who became Major League Baseball's highest-paid pitcher in 2009, is interviewed by reporters at a Florida training facility.

in the newsroom. In fact, working from remote bases has become a fairly common practice in sports journalism, just as it has in other professions. More and more writers are working from offices at their homes. Equipped with a laptop computer and smartphone, they can work from any remote location or while traveling and submit their material to editors online.

At major city dailies and sports magazines, some of the writers specialize in one or a few sports. Small city and town newspapers that employ only a handful of writers may assign one or two to cover all sports in the area. Some of the smallest weekly newspapers have only one reporter who covers sports in addition to general assignments.

Sportswriters' work has become mainly digitized. Today, most periodicals publish digital editions online. That means print reporters must write not just for daily, weekly, or monthly publication, but for Internet publication as well. Online content may need to be refreshed several times a day or week as new information becomes available.

Journalism is often fast-paced, with regular pressure. Reporters may work long hours with flexible schedules, including nights and weekends.

Sportswriters and editors face pressures unlike their counterparts on some of the other news desks. Because many of the events they cover end late at night, they're forced to rush frantically to meet deadlines. They also face pressure competing with writers for other periodicals. A missed deadline leaves the publication embarrassed in the eyes of readers. Reporters constantly vie for a news scoop or an exclusive interview with a hard-to-reach insider.

Some sportswriters are freelancers. They don't work full-time on a newspaper or magazine staff; rather, they accept assignments from editors of different periodicals. The upside of freelancing is the freedom to set your own hours and write for any and all publications that will buy your work. The downside is that it may be hard finding steady work. Monthly income is unpredictable—and in most cases, there are no health, retirement, or other employee benefits. Freelancers face extra pressure when juggling simultaneous projects for different editors.

A possible side career for sports journalists is to teach at local colleges. Some sportswriters parlay their experience and inside knowledge into full-length books: biographies of sports figures, exposés, or histories of sports dynasties. The job market for full-time book authors and feature writers is growing slowly compared to other professions, however. The BLS points out that there is strong competition for salaried writing jobs because the profession attracts many writers.

Many young people look forward to writing or shooting photographs for wire services, prominent periodicals, and sports magazines. For beginners, though, jobs with small newspapers are more likely to be had. The pay at first may be low, and the hours long. As they push for advancement, they will encounter more numerous and ever-stronger competition, especially as print periodicals downsize their staffs.

SPORTS COLUMNISTS

Sports columnists write opinion pieces and features to shed light on interesting aspects of a sports personality or topical issue. Columns are prized slots on sports pages, usually commanded by exceptional writers who have acquired followings of readers.

Famous sports columnists of the past have included Grantland Rice, Red Smith, Ring Lardner, and Shirley Povich. Popular latter-day columnists include Frank Deford, a *Sports Illustrated* columnist, author, and National Public Radio commentator; Bill Plaschke, writer for the *Los Angeles Times* and ESPN commentator; and Bob Ryan, noted basketball writer for the *Boston Globe* and regional sports talk-radio host.

On weekly newspapers, the opportunity to write a sports column gives a reporter or editor special exposure. Column space in some papers is awarded to respected retired journalists who still want to dabble in sportswriting. Columnists for dailies are usually reporters or editors. On some dailies, several reporters take turns contributing columns from day to day. Papers also feature nationally syndicated columnists.

Renowned sportswriter Frank Deford was presented the 2012 National Humanities Medal by President Barack Obama at a White House ceremony.

SPORTS EDITORS

Sports editors for daily newspapers plan the next day's sports section, make assignments, and manage the staff of writers, photographers, and columnists. They work with writers in developing story ideas. Editors are responsible for editing all of the articles for proper grammar, punctuation, and spelling. Although reporters are expected to ensure the accuracy of information in their articles, editors check behind them if questions arise. Editors do some rewriting themselves, but they may have to ask reporters to find additional information or rewrite some or all of a submission.

Editors allocate space for each story within the sports pages, including photos and design elements. They select wire stories and photos to include in the publication. Many editors lay out the sports pages. Some write features or columns several times a week.

Most editors work regular hours in the newspaper office. Increasingly, technology allows them to perform some or all of their work remotely.

Sports editors are usually promoted from the ranks of reporters. On a weekly newspaper, the sports editor almost invariably serves as a sportswriter. In some weekly production systems, the sports editor performs the page design and layout for the sports section. Small weeklies may employ just one sports staffer who is expected to write, edit, and lay out all of the sports news.

PHOTOGRAPHERS WHO SPECIALIZE

Most staff photographers for weekly newspapers and some for dailies cover a variety of news events, including sports. Those who shoot sports exclusively photograph different sports from season to season. Some professional freelancers, on the other hand, specialize.

Michael Clark, based in Santa Fe, New Mexico, is known internationally for his striking images of adventure sports—rock climbing, mountain biking, kayaking, and surfing, for example. He often goes to demanding extremes, sometimes risking his own safety to obtain spectacular angles and effects. He and his work have been featured in a number of professional photography journals. Clark is also noted for his landscape and travel pictures.

A freelance photographer might focus rewardingly on less-publicized sports. Czech photographer Vladimir Rys shoots myriad international sporting events, from soccer to swimming to the Special Olympics. He probably is best known for his dramatic images of Formula One car racing. Rys uses special effects to capture both action frames and striking still scenes that provoke viewers' curiosity and imagination.

Some sports photographers specialize geographically—for example, covering sports in their home cities. Jeanine Leech dreamed of being a sports photographer while a teenager absorbed in the pages of *Sports Illustrated*, to which her father subscribed. She obtained an associate's degree in visual communications from the Art Institute of Pittsburgh and began a career in graphic design. In 2005, she landed a post as assistant team photographer for the Pittsburgh Penguins NHL franchise. A few years later, she became lead sports photographer in Pittsburgh for the Icon Sports Media photo wire service. Leech is also well-known for her nature images.

The job market for print editors is unlikely to grow substantially in the foreseeable future, according to the BLS. The main reason for the stagnation is the increasing popularity of online publications.

SPORTS PHOTOGRAPHERS

Photography is a promising, rewarding area of print journalism. Sports photography is particularly exciting.

Sports photographers cover sporting events for newspapers, sports and news magazines, and wire services.

Photographers position themselves to take pictures along the sidelines at a National Football League preseason game. Notice the use of monopods, more easily portable than tripods, for stability.

Their schedules vary, depending on their assignments. The work involves travel to events, sometimes at long distances. A few obtain contracts, part-time or full-time, as staff photographers for athletic teams. Team photographers supply periodical editors with stock material that can be used anytime. They also furnish illustrations for advertising and marketing campaigns.

Shooters for newspapers and magazines revel in the fast pace of their work. The most successful also know the value of anticipation and patience. They position themselves precisely where they believe a climactic point in the action will occur. There, they wait—and hope—to capture the most exceptional split second. Disappointments are common.

On the sidelines of football games and other events, professional photographers can be seen with their long-lens cameras for capturing close-up action shots. An assortment of interchangeable lenses and other paraphernalia hangs from shoulder straps. The job can be physically demanding, especially at outdoor contests. Photographers may spend hours at a time standing, walking, and sprinting while shouldering heavy equipment.

Veteran photographers of fast-action sports have mastered a rich toolkit of techniques, such as panning and strip photography. They are experienced in using different cameras, lenses, filters, and other apparatus. When they go to work at any given assignment, they take along the items of equipment they know will serve them best.

The job market for photographers is growing at about the same pace as the national job average. The BLS observes that opportunities are becoming better for freelancers. More publications and organizations, to save costs, now engage freelancers rather than employ salaried photographers. Competition among freelance photographers is becoming intense.

A few professional photographers supplement their income teaching courses at colleges and tech schools, presenting workshops, and developing instructional courses and e-books.

WORRISOME JOB PROSPECTS

Careers as sportswriters and columnists for the print industry are exciting. But there are fewer openings today than there were twenty years ago. In a 2012 report, the Pew Research Center's Project for Excellence in Journalism declared that the newspaper industry "is neither dying nor assured of a stable future." A Pew survey found that between 1990 and 2009, the number of daily newspapers in the United States fell from 1,611 to 1,387. In 1989, there were almost fifty-seven thousand full-time editorial staff workers; the number plummeted by 27 percent by the end of 2010. The best news is that the rate of decline in newsroom workforce numbers seems to be slowing.

The explanation is twofold: 1) the Internet and 2) diminishing human attention spans. People today prefer to get up-to-the-minute news and information online ,rather than read it in a newspaper that went to press last night or a magazine published last week. Wherever they go, they are glued to their smartphones and tablet computers to stay constantly connected. When they settle in at home, they find it much more convenient and fast to check on televised news than read a newspaper.

Newspaper executives are not blind to the trend. They have been taking their periodicals online, selling digital subscriptions and advertisements. But in a 2013 *Forbes* article, Jeff Bertoluci cited statistics indicating that by and large, "publishers seem to be shedding print subscribers faster than they can replace them with readers of online, mobile, or replica editions."

Newspaper circulation has declined among papers large and small. That means those media platforms appeal less to advertisers. Print periodicals that also put their material online support this by selling onscreen ads. But they face competition on the Internet from other media: streaming TV and radio netcasts, digital directories, cable networks, and the onscreen offerings of "pure play" Internet companies such as Google. The resulting drop in advertising and subscription revenue means print newspapers and magazines are forced to reduce staff. Competition among job seekers has intensified.

Sports news careers offer a bit of a silver lining in this dark cloud. Sports articles, commentary, and photographs continue to draw readers to newspapers and magazines.

Broadcast sports media have not suffered in the same way as print media. Television and radio sports audiences are larger than ever. More sports events are covered now than ever before. Viewers expect to be able to choose from many different games and sports when they turn on the TV. Sports fans in transit rely on radio broadcasts to bring them the action moment by moment.

Chapter 5

HELPING AUDIENCES SEE AND HEAR THE EXCITEMENT

Careers in television and radio sports media can be especially stimulating. These professionals present the action to audiences in real time. They make the viewing or listening experience almost as meaningful as being at the event in person. In fact, given the wizardry of televised productions, many fans prefer to watch from the comfort of their homes.

Broadcast media companies employ media teams with varied talents. Some workers have the same titles as workers in print publishing and marketing or advertising, but with different roles. For example, broadcast reporters deliver their information in spoken rather than written words. Art directors in TV, video, and film production are in charge of set designs, working in collaboration with producers and directors.

Media specialists in broadcasting find jobs with local radio and television stations in both small and large media markets. Most of the top jobs are with networks or "super stations."

BROADCAST ANNOUNCERS

Announcers for local and area radio and television newscasts present all categories of news to listeners at regularly scheduled times throughout the day. Depending on the station's format, one radio announcer may read the hourly headlines of international, national, and statewide news, plus local sports results. Larger stations employ, in addition to news announcers, dedicated sports announcers and credentialed meteorologists.

Local television news stations typically employ teams of announcers working together in shifts: a news anchor or two coanchors, a meteorologist, and a sportscaster. The sports staff, besides the news desk announcer, may include one or more roving reporters assigned to report live from key games and to file backgrounder videos and interviews throughout the week. On the air, the announcer introduces the reporters' stories.

Some broadcast reporters and announcers are self-employed and work part-time. Self-employed broadcasters may record regular shows at home studios and sell them to television or radio stations.

Although some stations broadcast twenty-four hours a day, they might not hire late-night announcers. Much of the programming that airs in the early morning hours is prerecorded.

Regular television broadcasters work both inside soundproof studios and in the field. They help field reporters gather interviews and news. They write scripts to read on the air, but much of their work is done off the air. They keep up with breaking topics and research them to provide audiences with insightful coverage.

At some radio stations, announcers present commercials and make public service announcements. Even nationally familiar announcers for major networks periodically put in plugs for the network's prime-time programs.

Commentators, like announcers, must stay up to date and research the topics they will discuss. They sometimes prepare written scripts. Mainly, though, they engage in lively discussions. Color commentators at game broadcasts explain what just happened and why the play developed the way it did.

It may seem to audiences that sportscasters and commentators have cushy jobs. However, they work hard, often under stress. They don't merely show up on game day and lend their professional voices and sports expertise to provide entertaining

Commentators are busy inside a stadium press box during a game. Most of their work, though, involves research and interviews beforehand.

presentations. Those who appear on national television spend many hours the week before talking to players and coaches, studying videos of previous games, and discussing what to expect. They prepare themselves thoroughly. By game time, they truly can speak expertly about the game at hand, key players, coaching strategies, and each team's strengths and weaknesses.

In recent decades, all-sports cable television networks and radio talk shows have become very popular. Some radio stations are devoted almost exclusively to sports news and talk. Announcers comment on current sports news and issues. They conduct live interviews and moderate panel

The veteran on-air team members for *Sunday Night Football* take part in a panel discussion. From left: sideline reporter Michele Tafoya, analyst Chris Collinsworth, and play-by-play commentator Al Michaels.

discussions involving commentators—many of them former athletes—recognized as experts. They also host audience call-in shows. Well-known sports announcers frequently are invited to make appearances and give talks at public and private meetings and promotions.

Part-time and seasonal jobs are available to announcers at a local level. Public address announcers emcee events for the attending audience. They keep fans entertained as well as informed. Public address announcers must be thoroughly familiar with game rules and penalty signals.

The job market for television, radio, and public address system announcers will grow more slowly than the overall career average, the BLS anticipates. Improving technology and consolidation of stations will limit growth. Stations can now do more with fewer employees.

Competition among job candidates will heighten. Entry-level candidates increasingly will find themselves vying with experienced, popular announcers.

Entry-level broadcasting job candidates commonly go to work at small stations to acquire experience. There, they develop their broadcast personalities, gradually becoming more comfortable and engaging in their interactions with guests and audiences. Audience ratings among competing stations within a broadcast market are vital factors in an announcer's promotion prospects. Larger, better-paying companies look for on-air personalities who have proven they can build and keep a following.

"CYBER JOCKEYING": A JOB-CUTTING TREND

Radio and television stations have been looking for ways to cut costs. Technology helps them do so. The BLS explains, "Technology continues to increase the productivity of radio and television announcers and reduce the time required to edit material or do other off-air technical and production work."

One innovation that radio stations use is "cyber jockeying." Also called voice tracking, it is the development of a prerecorded program that combines an announcer's talk with commercials and other content. Each segment of the program can be a separate digital file, so production can be computerized. The program—which gives the impression of a live broadcast—can be presented during late-night and weekend shifts when no announcer is actually at the station. The process also enables the company to use material recorded by a professional announcer, perhaps a freelancer, who lives and works in a distant city.

With cyber jockeying, station owners require fewer staff members to provide "live" programming. In fact, the technology has eliminated many late-night shifts. Multiple stations commonly use material from the same announcer.

Advancement may occur within a broadcasting organization but more often involves a move to a different station or network. The BLS notes that the best opportunities are with larger organizations. "Because smaller market stations have smaller staff, advancement within the same radio or television station is unlikely. Rather, many radio and television announcers advance by relocating to a station in a larger market."

BROADCAST REPORTERS

Television and radio reporters conduct interviews and develop on-the-scene news reports. Most sports reporters' presentations are recorded for later broadcast. Sometimes, especially in the days and hours leading up to a major event, they report live.

Broadcast reporters perform daily tasks similar to those of print reporters:

- Establish contacts and relationships with sports personalities and experts who can give them information and ideas for interesting reports.
- Research subjects for reports that are assigned by their station or network's sports directors, or that they come up with themselves.
- Interview sources who can contribute to the report. A report may be edited to contain interview clips with one or more key sources. The reporter also conducts unrecorded interviews with others to obtain background information.
- Write scripts for the reports they will read on the air.

Broadcaster Jim Nance (*left*) interviews former NBA star Gary Payton at Payton's induction into the Naismith Memorial Basketball Hall of Fame. Payton later became a television analyst.

- Record voiceovers for TV reports, providing details and commentary to accompany video segments.
- Follow up on certain reports, if updates are appropriate.

For some news organizations, reporters edit their own interviews and create the finished report. While on assignment, they may create two or more variations of their report, to be aired at different times.

PRODUCERS AND DIRECTORS

Broadcast programming producers have overall responsibility for their shows, including budgets and staffing. Networks and stations in large broadcast markets have production staffs; an executive producer supervises assistant producers who are in charge of different aspects of a broadcast. Smaller operations are managed by a single producer.

Directors run the show as it is being presented in the studio or on location. They simultaneously direct engineering, technical, video/camera, and announcing personnel.

A REPORTER'S DIVERSE CAREER

Sports fans may know Holly Rowe best as a sidelines contributor at nationally televised college football games on ESPN. Her sports media career, though, is remarkably varied. She's reported on televised swimming competition, basketball, volleyball, track and field, and the FIFA Women's World Cup of association football (soccer). Rowe has even covered one of the more bizarre categories of "sports": the famous—or infamous—Running of the Bulls in Pamplona, Spain. From around the world, athletes and amateur daredevils convene there each year to prove their valiance. They try to outrace or dodge a herd of horned bulls let loose through the streets.

Rowe graduated from the University of Utah in 1991 with a degree in broadcast journalism. She wrote sports articles for college and county newspapers and obtained a year's internship with CBS Sports. She began telecasting women's college basketball games for Fox Sports in 1993 and since then has worked for different broadcast networks and organizations.

Joining the regular ESPN staff in 1998, she is now involved mainly in presentations of college football, college and professional basketball, and softball games. She has also written and produced sports documentaries and television features.

Producers and directors face daily stress to ensure each production is on schedule and well presented. Those who work on regular broadcast programs have generally consistent hours. Those whose teams cover on-site games and competitions have greatly variable schedules that may involve long, extended travel.

The BLS expects the job growth rate for producers and directors to hold steady at about the national career growth average. Although stations are consolidating, audiences seem to want more local programming.

CAMERA OPERATORS AND VIDEO EDITORS

Camera operators capture the action of sporting events on video. At major events, sports and news networks assign

Television camera crew members follow golfer Ai Miyazato during a championship tournament in California. Miyazato has been the LPGA's top-ranked player.

multiple camera operators to work from different angles. Directors coordinate their efforts. Editors usually work in the film industry, but some are employed to construct the contents for certain broadcast productions.

Camera operators and editors work closely with directors. They decide how best to approach the production and discuss video techniques, positions, and angles. For news conferences and studio interviews, operators pre-plan their setups and follow directors' guidance. Editors may condense and refine the footage before it is shown on TV. When shooting sports events, operators have to alter their setups to follow the action.

Electronic news gathering (ENG) operators cover breaking news. They may be sent to news locations on short notice. At the scene, they often have to act and react instantly. ENG operators often do their own editing on location before submitting their footage to the staff in the studio.

Operators select the best equipment for the job. Most work with at least one camera assistant. Assistants help find the most promising angles, set up cameras, and help keep the cameras steady and in focus. They help carry, maintain, and store equipment.

About a third of camera operators are self-employed. They work under contract with media organizations. Some operators and editors work in or near the cities where they live; others may travel extensively, transporting their heavy equipment. Broadcast camera operators assigned to a major sports event work long hours at a time.

Beginning operators and editors usually start as assistants, often at small television stations, and work their way up to regular roles. Eventually, some of them become directors and producers. For the foreseeable future, the BLS expects little growth in the job market for camera operators and editors.

BROADCAST AND SOUND ENGINEERING TECHNICIANS

While announcers and broadcast reporters concentrate on presenting information to television and radio audiences, an unseen, unheard staff works to ensure technical quality. Broadcast and sound engineering technicians set up and run complex electrical and digital audio-video equipment. They usually work regular schedules inside station or network studios. Those who cover sports events may work outdoors, sometimes in adverse weather. The work may involve heavy lifting and climbing antennas and poles. Workers are taught safety standards for handling electronic equipment and cabling.

Some technicians are self-employed, working under contract for broadcasting and sports organizations. Routine tasks include the following:

- Operating audio-video equipment during a broadcast. This includes monitoring and adjusting volume and display settings to constantly present the best sound and image quality. It also includes ensuring precise synchronization of video action with announcers' voices and other sounds.

- Recording the programs.

- Installing and repairing or replacing sound and video equipment in studios or other broadcast locations.

A broadcast camera operator braves high winds at a golf tournament in Hawaii. Photographers and camera crews sometimes work in hazardous situations.

- Setting up and taking down equipment for game broadcasts.

- Providing digital files of broadcasts and recordings for editors.

- Keeping records of broadcasts, recordings, and equipment use.

Technicians at small stations may perform a variety of jobs. At large stations and networks, individual technicians specialize. Some of the specialists include these:

- Chief engineers and field supervisors supervise the staff of technicians. They are responsible for equipment maintenance.

- Audio and video equipment technicians set up and operate the audio-video equipment needed for a broadcast. Equipment includes microphones, speakers, sound and mixing boards, video screens and monitors, projectors, lights, cables, and wires.

- Broadcast technicians set up and work with precision sound and video equipment. They master instruments that regulate audio clarity, signal strength, and color ranges. Broadcast technicians run radio and TV transmitters. They edit recordings, using computer software.

- Sound and recording engineers synchro-
nize, record, and mix sound elements for
media productions, including sporting
events. Some of the sounds are recorded

An audio engineer inside a studio works on a digital soundtrack for an NFL Films
presentation. Computer software enables technicians to combine multiple sound files.

at different times and places; the separate sound files are combined digitally into a multilayered file.

- Recording engineers specialize in operating audio and video recording equipment, including special effects technology.

- Sound mixers produce soundtracks for network TV programs and films.

- Field technicians specialize in running portable equipment for broadcast assignments away from the studio.

Technical staff must be on their toes constantly. The entire televised or audio production can succeed brilliantly or turn embarrassing, depending on their performance.

During a college football conference championship game telecast in 2007, a sideline journalist reported to her upstairs announcers and TV viewers that one of the quarterbacks was visibly exasperated by the way things were going. The live report was accidentally plugged into the stadium's public address system. The puzzled player found himself being analyzed for the fans attending the game.

Technicians entering the job market begin at small stations. Networks and large stations hire only experienced and specialist technicians. New opportunities for technicians will arise as radio and TV stations periodically upgrade their equipment to improve sound and video quality. Fast-changing technology requires technicians to learn new equipment frequently.

The BLS expects career openings to expand at an average rate, although job growth is stagnating for sound engineering technicians. Again, station consolidation and technological advances are the main reasons.

Chapter 6

MAKING SPORTS NEWS VIRAL

Millions of sports fans now spend most of their sports time online. They still devote some free time to reading sports magazines and the sports sections of

Jean Afterman, assistant general manager of the New York Yankees, checks her mobile phone during a game. Afterman was an actress, player agent, and lawyer before becoming a baseball executive.

newspapers. They still take in games and talk shows on television and radio. But more and more, they're seen with their noses buried in their mobile devices—even while viewing games on TV.

The reason is that online, they can get exactly what they want, instantly. Moreover, they can get it wherever they happen to be. A few taps on their smartphone screens keeps them up-to-the-minute on every game-day score. They can watch their choice of live telecasts on tablet computers while riding in a car or sitting on a park bench. They can read updated sports articles at online periodical and blog sites. They can view video highlights of ongoing events, zoom in, and replay the video clips at will. They can share the latest photos and videos while chatting with friends remotely.

The ability to share online content so quickly has given sports information a viral quality. Within minutes, a posted blog report, photo, or video clip can spread to millions of connected Internet users around the globe.

Most of the sports content online is available for audiences to view or read at no cost. At the same time, paying jobs in Internet sports media are on the rise. Media organizations and individuals have learned to generate revenue with their Internet content. Online sports media channels need professionals with diverse skills.

NEWSPAPERS AND MAGAZINES TAKE TO THE INTERNET

Print publishers began to worry about their future in the 1990s, as consumers began turning to the Internet for information and news. They realized that the Net offers readers a tremendous advantage in timeliness. Developing news around the world can be reported online almost immediately. It can be updated minute by minute.

Grudgingly but steadily, print newspapers and magazines began publishing articles in Internet versions of their periodicals. It might seem that in doing so, they are giving away valuable content. Online publication removes the incentive for readers to pay print subscription fees.

Publishers have found several ways to generate revenue with online publishing. For example, the free online version of their periodical might present shortened versions of the print articles—or only teasers, a paragraph or two to grab readers' attention. To obtain the full contents, online visitors must pay to subscribe to a full Internet edition.

Also, publishers sell advertisements that appear with the online articles. Online advertising is not cheap. Publishers have begun to recover much of the revenue they're losing from dwindling print advertising sales.

PUTTING THE WRITTEN WORD ONLINE

Many of the jobs performed for print publications are being adapted for online publishing projects. Today, print reporting mingles with Internet reporting. Researchers and writers develop content for Web sites and blog posts. There is an increasing need for online writing talent. There also is a need for experienced editors to refine Web content.

Sports fans still wait to read accounts of today's games in tomorrow's newspapers. Meanwhile, millions go to the Web within hours or minutes after a game ends to find full reports and commentary at the newspapers' online sites. Besides filing their main reports, sportswriters are posting "notebook" blogs, offering a better understanding of the game with their personal observations.

The Internet allows sportswriters to interact directly with their readers via blogs as well as their Facebook walls and Twitter feeds. In this way, they obtain instantaneous reader feedback while promoting their newspapers.

In a 2012 report, the Pew Research Center's Project for Excellence in Journalism noted: "Newspaper organizations have cranked up their Twitter and Facebook efforts, finding social media both a means to drive traffic to their stories and a reporting resource to find sources quickly during breaking news events."

Digital subscriptions to periodicals that once were print-only are catching on. The *Wall Street Journal*, for example, has some half million digital subscribers. If they can generate online subscriptions and advertising, publishers realize tremendous advantages in the digital age. They save costs on paper printing and distribution while contributing to a greener planet. Most importantly for their readers, they can update news articles throughout the day as new information becomes available.

Media companies are not alone in providing audiences with online sports content. Freelance sportswriters, fans, athletes, and journalism students operate sports-related blogs. For blogging novices, services like SportsBlog.com offer to help create and promote new projects.

Broadcast professionals are also finding ways to use their experience and knowledge in Web work. Sports podcasts have become popular, as have sports-oriented Internet radio projects.

Some analysts believe the future of media is online. Regardless, practically everyone interested in a sports media career will need to acquire technology smarts.

PHOTOGRAPHERS TAKE ADVANTAGE OF THE INTERNET

Most photographers now shoot with digital cameras rather than film. They transfer their images from their cameras to computers and electronic storage devices. After

Sports on Film is the online gallery founded by photographer Brian Westerholt. It features sports photographs at every level, from youth to pro.

editing them with Photoshop or other software, they can send them to publishers quickly online.

Many professional sports photographers maintain Web sites displaying onscreen portfolios. Some offer catalogs of digital images for sale. The Internet has made it very easy to market images this way. Sales can be made and images delivered to buyers almost instantly.

GENERATING PUBLICITY ONLINE

Marketing and public relations professionals for sports organizations now distribute much of their information and publicity material online. Advertising specialists, too, find online job opportunities because advertising is primarily what makes online publishing profitable.

The Internet opens new opportunities for art directors and graphic designers working in marketing/PR firms as well as in newsrooms. Graphic designers create illustrations and find photographs and video/audio files to make online presentations dynamic. The BLS, in its *Occupational Outlook Handbook,* states: "With the increased use of the Internet, designers will be needed to create designs and images for portable devices, websites, electronic publications, and video entertainment media."

New online opportunities likewise are expected for art directors, even as they decline at traditional print periodicals. The BLS explains: "Rather than focusing on the print layout of photographs and text, art directors for newspapers and magazines will design Web pages that incorporate a variety of photographs, illustrations, graphic designs, and text images."

INTERPRETING THE NUMBERS: STATISTICIANS

A unique job category in sports media is statistics. Statisticians collect and analyze data, primarily numbers. They present their reports typically in the forms of graphs, charts, and tables. Statisticians command well-paying

Los Angeles Clippers basketball coach Vinny Del Negro studies statistics during a game. Accurate statistics are vital to the success of sports programs.

jobs in government and numerous areas of business, including sports.

Sports fans are riveted on the numbers concerning their favorite teams, rival teams, and individual athletes. Athletes keep track of their personal stats to measure their progress or slippage. Coaching staffs use statistics to evaluate players. In large part, statistics tell the tale in scouting reports.

Sportswriters and broadcasters often muse that an athlete or team "looks good on paper"—statistically, that is. Today, it may be more accurate to say "looks good onscreen." The Internet has become an important medium for statisticians to report their information and for fans and researchers to find it.

Statistics are ingrained in the reporting of practically every sport. Analysts today reach to extraordinary depths in critiquing performances and trends. They go far beyond free-throw averages in basketball and yards-per-completion in football. To people unfamiliar with certain sports, some categories of statistics seem hardly meaningful—for example, the percentage of a professional golfer's drives that land on the fairway.

Some statistics bring to light amusing nuggets of sports trivia. Here are a few examples:

- Prices that sports items once owned by celebrities have brought at auctions.

- The number of possible plays in every nine-inning baseball game (more than twelve million).

- The greatest height discrepancy between a pitcher and batter in professional baseball (Jon Rauch, standing 6 feet 11 inches [2.11 m], pitching against Jose Altuve, 5 feet 5 inches [1.65 m].

- The average number of cowhides used in making the NFL's footballs for one season (about three thousand).

- The number of National Hockey League players to score five goals in one game (forty-four).

Statisticians usually work full-time at computers in offices. Overtime work may be required when they are nearing contractual deadlines. Advancement opportunities naturally are greater for those with higher degrees. Some statisticians become consultants.

Job growth prospects for statisticians will be good in coming years—as promising as or better than the career average, the BLS projects. "Growth will result from more widespread use of statistical analysis to make informed decisions. In addition, the large increase in available data from the Internet will opcn up new areas for analysis."

Chapter 7
CREATING A BUZZ

Success in business doesn't just happen. Most businesses actively promote themselves. They try to appeal to consumers directly. They also connect indirectly via news and entertainment media.

Sports organizations and high-profile athletes are no different. They hire public relations, marketing, and advertising professionals to develop and broaden their reputations. The job of the PR/marketing professional is to generate effective, positive publicity and advertising for the client; to run interference if negative news breaks; and to keep the client in the public eye.

Some sports organizations contract with outside advertising and marketing firms to handle their promotional efforts. Within those firms, staffers in different roles (designers, copywriters, technical or sales personnel, and so forth) at different levels may find their work focused exclusively on sports. Others are assigned to a variety of client projects in different businesses and industries.

PUBLIC RELATIONS MANAGERS AND SPECIALISTS

Public relations professionals focus on daily press and community relations for their employers/clients. They serve as contact points when news reporters want to contact the sports organization. They provide requested information and put the media in touch with appropriate individuals inside the organization. Also, they help athletes and others in the organization communicate effectively with the press. When controversies arise—as they frequently do in sports—public relations professionals work to contain the fallout.

Specialists research and write press releases and feature articles to submit to print and broadcast media. They develop personality profiles and human-interest stories about athletes, coaches, owners, and others, and pitch the stories to magazine, newspaper, and newsletter editors. They're also engaged in ongoing campaigns that may include team programs, booklets, profiles, and whitepapers. Sometimes they're called on to draft speeches for their employers.

Press releases developed by PR specialists sometimes turn into headline news. A study by Jim Macnamara, an Australian educator and author focusing on media topics, tracked press releases distributed by public relations

Patrick Smythe, executive director of media relations for the Denver Broncos, talks with quarterback Peyton Manning at a training camp just before a press conference.

firms. It showed that about 30 percent provided the fodder for news reports.

Managers identify primary audiences and develop strategies for connecting with them. They oversee the work of staff specialists. They also work closely with marketing and advertising departments to make sure all promotional projects are in keeping with the organization's purpose and brand. The brand is the organization's visual identity, instantly recognized by the public. The brand includes, for example, a team's nickname, colors, emblem, and mascot. It may also include a catchy slogan or audio jingle.

Some days, PR workers keep regular office hours. Often, however, they are expected to attend after-hours and weekend events. Travel may be involved. There is frequent stress, especially for workers assigned to multiple clients or projects at the same time. They may have to work long hours to meet their deadlines.

Growth in the public relations career field is expected to be strong, as is competition among job seekers. The BLS predicts a 21 percent PR job growth rate for the decade 2010–2020.

MEETING AND EVENT PLANNERS

Promotions managers and staff strive to generate publicity or revenue for the organization with special incentives: "meet the press" and other public appearances by athletes or coaches, ticket discounts or giveaways, contests to energize fans and prospective new fans, and the like.

Meeting and event planners handle all the details of an event. Tasks include selecting the site and time, helping choose speakers, formulating the agenda, planning receptions, coordinating responsibilities with on-site staff, arranging lodging and transportation for participants and attendees, ensuring there are no embarrassing omissions among the invitees, and securing all necessary gear and accessories. They must make sure the location is ideal and everything the presenting organization needs is provided.

Erin Gamroth, director of public relations and special events for Special Olympics of Wyoming, works on a logo for the organization's Web site.

Typical facilities, equipment, and conveniences are furnished conference rooms; press rooms with complete, organized press kits and reliable communication connections; microphone and speaker systems with safe, secured cabling; digital presentation systems including computers, software, and projection screens; constantly staffed registration and help desks; coffee and refreshment areas; and information packets suggesting local attractions, dining, and entertainment for visitors.

Event planners also manage the cost of the affair. They find the best prices for rental equipment and operation, photography, food service, and other needs. At the conclusion of the event, they perform satisfaction surveys with attendees and meet with the sponsors for debriefings.

Planners keep regular office hours—except during an event. They must be on the scene long before the agenda begins and remain until after it's over, making sure it runs smoothly at every stage. The pace is usually fast as they oversee the meeting staff and help resolve problems on the fly.

The BLS expects careers for meeting and event planners to grow by 44 percent between 2010 and 2020. This is much greater than the average growth rate in other career areas. The reasons, the BLS explains, are increased globalization and the recognition that professionally planned meetings are essential.

The bureau cautions, however, that competition is intensifying since "the occupation usually attracts more applicants than job openings."

ADVERTISING AND MARKETING SPECIALISTS AND MANAGERS

While public relations professionals maintain a positive day-to-day image for athletes and organizations, marketing and ad specialists look for new ideas and develop campaigns to promote a brand and generate a buzz. Major sports organizations or the agencies that represent them employ multifaceted marketing and advertising staffs. The job of these professionals is to constantly generate new interest in the client, whether it's a college or amateur program or professional organization. Workers collaborate with staff in other departments, as well as with the public and sports media.

Marketing managers confer with the sports administration to develop promotional campaigns. They decide the best media to use (television/radio, print, billboards, online social media, and so forth) for launching them. Advertising or marketing managers negotiate advertising contracts. Within their departments, marketing and advertising managers oversee design and other production professionals, inspecting ad mock-ups, videos, Web presentations, and other projects.

Thierry Weil, marketing director of the International Federation of Association Football, appears at a media briefing to announce host cities for the Confederations Cup.

SPORTS PUBLICISTS

Marketing, public relations, and advertising professionals who serve the general market sometimes "back into" sports media work. Elaine Gillespie, who operates a marketing and PR firm in South Carolina, knew little about sports marketing until one of her clients referred to her a friend—a famous professional wrestler. The celebrity happened to be looking for a media representative. After an hour interview, he asked Gillespie to handle his publicity.

Her immediate reaction was amazement. She'd never before represented a sports professional, and she told him frankly she wasn't sure how to go about it. He, though, was confident he'd found just the right publicist.

She ultimately took the contract and booked him for hundreds of public and media appearances in the coming years. Gillespie reflects, "This was a strange extension of advertising and public relations, but somehow it all worked hand in hand."

Gillespie majored in studio art in college. Entering the career world, she became bored as a graphic artist for an agency. She started her own agency and expanded it to provide marketing and public relations services. "Eventually," she explains, "I realized that I could provide much more to my clients than a graphic designer."

A valuable nugget of advice from Gillespie to freelancers and independent PR/marketing professionals: be open and attentive to surprising opportunities that might present themselves.

Advertising and marketing leaders involved with sports organizations work full-time; some average fifty hours or longer per week. Out-of-town travel is often required. They should be prepared to manage stress when meeting project deadlines.

To land mid- or high-level jobs, employees need fundamental experience in how each business works. Many marketing and advertising managers get their start as sales representatives, purchasing agents, and product demonstrators.

Career prospects are bright for advertising, marketing, and promotions managers in varied areas—and competition is expected to be strong. Every sports organization that relies on revenue to keep itself going must create a continual buzz to maintain and increase fan enthusiasm and public awareness of its successes.

For those interested in an advertising/marketing career, the BLS points out that ad and promotions managers will be hired particularly to manage media campaigns online. Also, with the growth in Internet advertising, digital expertise is critical for ad managers to advance.

GRAPHIC DESIGNERS AND ART DIRECTORS

The basic role of graphic designers is to make information and ideas look good in print and onscreen. The BLS summarizes this way: "Graphic designers create visual concepts, by hand or using computer software, to communicate ideas that inspire, inform, or captivate consumers." After graduating from college with design degrees, young artists should expect to work one to three years acquiring experience on a variety of projects. They can advance to such positions as senior or lead designer, art director, or creative director.

Art directors for print and online media come up with the overall design of editorial and publicity presentations. They direct designers or teams of designers, illustrators,

Art and design teams plan and create a variety of visual elements to promote sports organizations. Some staffs include art directors, graphic artists, illustrators, and photographers.

and photographers in bringing the concept to reality. Most art directors have at least three years of experience in design, illustration, photography, writing/editing, or a combination.

Art directors and graphic designers usually work inside the offices of marketing and advertising firms. Some are in positions where they can telecommute. About a third are self-employed; they perform freelance work for different agencies or operate solo design studios, often home-based.

The work of art directors involves:

- Meeting with clients to discuss project objectives and artistic styles;
- Setting a budget for the project;
- "Concepting" the project (advertising campaign, brochure, directory, and so on) and deciding generally how to depict it effectively;
- Choosing from among the design elements to use, such as artwork, photographs, and typefaces;
- Directing, reviewing, and approving the work of the design staff;
- Working with other departments and staff, including copywriters, copy editors, and sales professionals;
- Presenting the completed project to the client for approval and directing the staff in effecting requested changes.

Routine tasks of designers include:

- Meeting with the art director and/or client to learn the nature and scope of the project;
- Suggesting ideas and strategies for communicating visually with the target audience;
- Creating images and finding photographs to illustrate the project effectively;
- Working with typefaces and sizes, images, colors, charts, tables, lists, and other elements and laying out the project;
- Reviewing the design to ensure there are no omissions or mistakes;
- Presenting the drafted work to the art director and/or client;
- Incorporating requested changes.

Art directors and graphic designers keep standard business hours some days but frequently work early and late to stay on schedule. They sometimes travel to meet with clients.

The BLS projects jobs for graphic designers to grow approximately 13 percent during this decade, about the average for all career growth. The BLS advises that job competition will increase because thousands of talented young people are interested in careers as artists and graphic designers. Designers experienced in Web site design and other interactive media will have the best opportunities for employment and advancement.

The market for art directors is expected to improve more slowly. As in the graphic design market, job growth probably will be strongest in Internet media.

Some experienced art directors and graphic designers teach courses at schools and colleges.

ONLINE NETWORKING NOW DRIVES PUBLICITY

The Internet has changed communications dramatically, worldwide. Some media observers enthuse that we are becoming a well-connected global society.

For sports media workers, the Internet definitely has impacted the way they perform their daily work. It's a matter of getting the public's attention—connecting with an audience, using the audience's choice of connecting platforms. PR and marketing specialists still communicate regularly with print and broadcast media contacts by phone. But they've also woven valuable new "webs" online for spreading information. Today's sports marketing campaigns involve Web sites, e-mail, social media, blogs, live chats, and other online avenues.

Twenty-first-century marketers and publicists have networks of coworkers and other routine contacts. They communicate by texting, e-mailing, and video chatting. They have separate webs of media contacts, communicating in the same ways. And they devote small segments of their work time to interacting with the public, answering questions and offering comments on behalf of their employer organizations. Social networking technology makes possible "relational marketing," almost in real time. It lets fans and others know that someone inside the sports organization really is "listening" to what they have to say.

Mari Smith, a social media marketing consultant and author of *The New Relationship Marketing*, has pointed out that a marketer in the new era "can't afford to be a one-way broadcast channel."

Chapter 8
INTO THE FUTURE

The mushrooming popularity of sports in modern culture is phenomenal. It offers a diversion from the stresses of life. It also presents vibrant news topics, even in Third World countries. Interest in sports has accelerated throughout the last century, propelled by new media and technology. Because of that, career prospects in sports media are bright, although opportunities in certain career areas are more limited than in others.

For a broad sampling of current job listings, students can search the different job boards on the Internet. For more focused results, visit the Web sites of specific sports media and look for posted job openings. Students interested in sports broadcasting careers, for instance, might visit the job sections posted online at Fox Sports, ESPN, and major news broadcasting networks, or at area television and radio station Web sites. Those who yearn to write sports articles and columns for magazines and newspapers should investigate the staff credentials and job boards at some of the publications' Web sites.

An interesting searching ground is among the job openings for sports organizations, including professional and minor leagues and colleges. They hire such media professionals as public relations and marketing specialists. New media job titles are being created. A good example is that of social media coordinator. Social media specialists are assigned to perform such tasks as interacting with fans and generating lively content for the team's Web site, Facebook page, and blog.

EXPANDING OPPORTUNITIES FOR WOMEN

In the twenty-first century, women's athletics are steadily becoming as interesting to general audiences as male competitions. That makes those sports quite lucrative for sports publishing and broadcasting companies. But even before female sports events made their way into primetime viewing schedules, women had begun to make inroads into sports media careers.

The movement is bolstered by the advent of media organizations such as the Association for Women in Sports Media (AWSM). The AWSM, founded in 1987, mentors professional women and sponsors college internships and scholarships for students interested in this career field.

Holly Rowe interviews Skylar Diggins after the University of Notre Dame basketball standout was drafted by the Tulsa Shock of the WNBA.

TV sports networks have recognized the particular value of women media professionals. ESPN, for example, launched espnW in 2011. ESPN took notice of the statistic that women comprise a sizeable segment of its viewers. The new espnW brand of the network was developed to appeal especially to the female audience, providing broadened opportunities for women interested in sports media.

A CRUCIAL NEW TOOL: TECHNOLOGY

Career counselors emphasize the importance of mastering communications technology for media career aspirants.

Tools of the trade for broadcast technicians and engineers include state-of-the-art equipment. Photographers need top-of-the-line digital cameras and accessories. Journalists use mobile computers and devices and take advantage of file sharing and collaboration technology.

In addition, professionals in diverse career categories are employing social media in their work. Reporters sometimes conduct interviews via video chat and e-mail. Marketers and event planning teams in different locales can meet in teleconferences. Press conferences can be attended online by thousands of sports journalists located thousands of miles from the conference site. PR workers and publicists tweet news nuggets and schedule information on behalf of their clients.

Sports marketing and PR professionals today engage not just in "transactional marketing" (pitching favorable news items to the press) but also "relational marketing" (opening lines of direct communication with fans). Publicity campaigns include daily interaction with the public in Twitter and Facebook exchanges, chats, e-texts and e-mail, and blog posts and comments. Publicists recognize that citizens of the twenty-first century are spending much more time online and less time reading printed magazines and newspapers. Some media industry watchers believe that within the next decade or two, print literature will become almost obsolete.

WOMEN JOIN THE SPORTS PRESS GANG

Women held relatively few sports journalism jobs until the late 1900s. Today, female sportswriters, TV and radio commentators, bloggers, and technical staffers are not at all out of the ordinary. On television screens, they include sports desk anchors as well as sideline reporters.

Many women sports journalists give credit for these advances to Title IX under the federal Education Amendments of 1972. The legislation states that no one, on the basis of sex, can be "excluded from participation in, be denied the benefits of, or be subjected to discrimination under" any educational program that receives federal government funds. Backers of the policy note that during the last forty years, it has resulted in numerous scholarships and other opportunities for female athletes. That, in turn, has spurred the increase in women sportswriters and broadcast professionals.

As ESPN commentator Holly Rowe has explained: "Title IX has been a huge factor in the growth of women in broadcasting because there are a lot more women's sports on television. All the women's games are on. And that's awesome because women growing up in this era think it's normal to be on TV."

TELECOMMUTING SPORTS MEDIA WORKERS

For years, sports correspondents and photographers have worked remotely, writing reports and taking photographs locally and submitting them to distant publishers via e-mail and electronic file transfers. Meanwhile, sports commentators have made careers for themselves as professional bloggers.

This trend bodes well for young career hopefuls. They may find entry-level opportunities if they are seriously

A journalist holding a tablet computer participates in an interview with a South Korean gymnast who just arrived in London for the 2012 Summer Olympics.

developing interests and skills in digital photography or if they can write concise, informative reports from remote events and can meet a paper's deadline.

KEYS TO SUCCESS

The sports media job market is increasingly competitive. Job candidates who have focused on a specific role, bringing with them experience and targeted educational training, are in the best positions.

The likelihood of advancement in a sports media career depends mainly on the worker's performance at any given level. As in all professions, industriousness is key. Employees who offer to take on additional tasks and look for innovative ways to improve their work should expect to move ahead.

COLLEGE AND UNIVERSITY PROGRAMS IN SPORTS MEDIA

Most sports media professionals, depending on their work, hold degrees in areas such as journalism, communications, English, art, graphic design, and technical studies. Degree programs in these varied fields are offered at hundreds of U.S. colleges and universities.

Few higher institutions offer degrees specifically in sports media, but the numbers of curricula have been increasing with the heightened public interest in sports. Other schools offer communications-related degrees with concentrations in sports media.

Arizona State University, Phoenix, Arizona: bachelor of arts in business, with a concentration in sports and media studies.

Boston University, Boston, Massachusetts: master of science in journalism program, with a concentration in sports reporting.

Bradley University, Peoria, Illinois: undergraduate degree in sports communication.

Centennial College, Toronto, Ontario: post graduate certificate program in sports journalism.

Centralia College, Centralia, Washington:

media studies program includes an associate in arts degree in sports announcing and production.

Florida State University, Tallahassee, Florida: undergraduate program in media production includes an optional emphasis in sports media.

Full Sail University, Winter Park, Florida: bachelor of science program in sports marketing and media.

Indiana University, Indianapolis and Bloomington, Indiana: bachelor of science major in kinesiology, sports marketing, and management; master of arts degree in sports journalism.

Ithaca College, Ithaca, New York: bachelor of science in sports media.

Montclair State University, Montclair, New Jersey: bachelor of arts degree in television and digital media, with a sports media and journalism concentration.

New England School of Communications, Bangor, Maine: bachelor of science in media studies program, with a sports journalism concentration.

Northwest Missouri State University, Maryville, Missouri: bachelor of science program in mass media, with an emphasis on sports media.

Oklahoma State University, Stillwater, Oklahoma: bachelor of science program in sports media.

Penn State University, University Park, Pennsylvania: certificate program in sports journalism from the John Curley Center for Sports Journalism.

Syracuse University, Syracuse, New York: sports communications emphasis.

University of Iowa, Iowa City, Iowa: bachelor of arts in sports studies.

University of North Carolina, Chapel Hill, North Carolina: sports certificate from the School of Journalism and Mass Communication.

University of Southern California/Annenberg, Los Angeles, California: minor in sports media studies.

University of Texas at Austin, Austin, Texas: bachelor of science in communication, with a concentration in sports and media.

Valparaiso University, Valparaiso, Indiana: master of science in sports media degree.

Western Kentucky University, Bowling Green, Kentucky: master of science program in sports media and branding.

A CAREER IN SPORTS MEDIA AT A GLANCE

Career paths in sports media include the following.

ADVERTISING, PROMOTIONS, AND MARKETING MANAGERS

ACADEMICS

- Bachelor's degree

EXPERIENCE

- Advertising, promotion, marketing, or sales

- Digital experience

CAREER PATHS

- Managers work in agencies or within organizations.

DUTIES AND RESPONSIBILITIES

- Plan ad, promotional, or marketing campaigns

- Meet with clients

- Work with art directors, sales representatives, and financial staff

ANNOUNCERS

ACADEMICS

- High school diploma for public address announcers

- Bachelor's degree for radio and television announcers

EXPERIENCE

- Work at college radio or television stations

CAREER PATHS

- Most announcers begin work at small stations.

- With acquired experience and followings, they may advance to large stations or networks.

DUTIES AND RESPONSIBILITIES

- Present sports news

- Announce action at games

- Provide commentary

- Interview athletes, coaches, and other sources

ART DIRECTORS AND GRAPHIC DESIGNERS

ACADEMICS

- Bachelor's degree

EXPERIENCE

- Graphic design, illustration, copyediting, photography, or related tasks

CAREER PATHS

- Directors and designers work for advertising and public relations firms.

- Some work for print publishers.

- Large organizations may hire their own art and design staffs.

DUTIES AND RESPONSIBILITIES

- Develop the visual approach for a project

- Create art, layout, and other visual elements

BROADCAST AND SOUND ENGINEERING TECHNICIANS

ACADEMICS

- High school diploma, associate's degree, or vocational certificate
- Bachelor's degree for chief engineer jobs

EXPERIENCE

- Worsk with various equipment on broadcast teams

CAREER PATHS

- Begin work for small radio or television station.
- With experience, advance to larger station or network.
- Become supervisory technician or chief engineer.

DUTIES AND RESPONSIBILITIES

- Set up and operate equipment for radio and TV broadcasts
- Maintain equipment

FILM AND VIDEO EDITORS AND CAMERA OPERATORS

ACADEMICS

- Bachelor's degree

EXPERIENCE

- On-the-job training
- Assistant roles

CAREER PATHS

- Video editors and camera operators work for broadcast stations or networks, in studios and on location.

DUTIES AND RESPONSIBILITIES

- Record the action at sports events
- Record interviews and press conferences
- Edit recorded video
- Work with producers and directors to create a final presentation

MEETING, CONVENTION, AND EVENT PLANNERS

ACADEMICS

- Bachelor's degree

EXPERIENCE

- Experience in event planning and on-site work and management

- Familiarity with virtual meeting software and social media

CAREER PATHS

- Event planners are hired by organizations or their marketing/PR agencies to plan and coordinate special events.

DUTIES AND RESPONSIBILITIES

- Coordinate all aspects of meetings and similar events

- Choose event locations

- Arrange transportation

PHOTOGRAPHERS

ACADEMICS

- No postsecondary education for entry-level assignments

- Bachelor's degree for photojournalists

EXPERIENCE

- Experience with different types of cameras and accessory equipment

- Computerized photo-editing familiarity

CAREER PATHS

- Photographers are hired by newspapers, magazines, marketing/PR firms, and sports organizations.

DUTIES AND RESPONSIBILITIES

- Produce and preserve images that tell a story or record an event

- Organize and edit digital photos

- Provide image files to media editors or organizations

PRODUCERS AND DIRECTORS

ACADEMICS

- Degree in broadcasting or communications

EXPERIENCE

- Experience with broadcast equipment and technology

CAREER PATHS

- Sports producers and directors work for television and radio stations and networks.

DUTIES AND RESPONSIBILITIES

- Oversee and direct broadcast, film, and other visual productions, in studios or on location.

PUBLIC RELATIONS MANAGERS AND SPECIALISTS

ACADEMICS

- Bachelor's degree

EXPERIENCE

- Writing and speaking experience
- Social media familiarity

CAREER PATHS

- PR personnel work in agencies or in PR departments within organizations.

DUTIES AND RESPONSIBILITIES

- Create and maintain a favorable public image for a client
- Write material for media releases
- Plan and/or direct PR campaigns
- Raise funds for client organizations

REPORTERS, CORRESPONDENTS, AND BROADCAST NEWS ANALYSTS

ACADEMICS

- Bachelor's degree

EXPERIENCE

- Begin work at small newspapers or broadcast stations

- With experience, advance to larger media organizations

CAREER PATHS

- Reporters, correspondents, and broadcast news analysts work for newspapers, magazines, television/radio stations, or Web media.

DUTIES AND RESPONSIBILITIES

- Inform the public about sports news and events

STATISTICIANS

ACADEMICS

- Bachelor's or higher degree

EXPERIENCE

- Computer skills

- Statistical analysis

- Problem solving

CAREER PATHS

- Statisticians work for media and other organizations, usually inside offices, to gather and organize data.

DUTIES AND RESPONSIBILITIES

- Use mathematical techniques to analyze and interpret data and draw conclusions

WRITERS, AUTHORS, AND EDITORS

ACADEMICS

- Bachelor's degree

EXPERIENCE

- Computer familiarity

- Publication in student and local newspapers

CAREER PATHS

- Writers, authors, and editors work for newspapers, magazines, advertising and marketing firms, broadcast media, and Web publishers.

DUTIES AND RESPONSIBILITIES

- Research and write original content

- Edit and proofread written copy

ADVERTISING, PROMOTIONS, AND MARKETING MANAGERS

SIGNIFICANT POINTS

- Travel may be required.

- Many managers work extra hours.

- Strong job market competition is expected.

NATURE OF THE WORK

Advertising, promotions, and marketing managers plan programs to generate interest in a product or service. They work with art directors, sales agents, and financial staff members.

TRAINING

Most managers have degrees in advertising, journalism, or related fields.

OTHER QUALIFICATIONS

Experience may be required in advertising, promotion, marketing, or sales. Qualities include analytical skills, creativity, decision-making skills, interpersonal skills, and management skills.

ADVANCEMENT

Workers with digital experience have the best advancement prospects.

JOB OUTLOOK

Employment of advertising, promotions, and marketing managers is expected to grow 14 percent from 2010 to 2020, as fast as the average for all occupations. Advertising, promotions, and marketing will continue to be essential for organizations as they seek to maintain and expand their share of the market.

WORK ENVIRONMENT

Advertising, promotions, and marketing managers typically work in offices close to those of top executives. The jobs of advertising, promotions, and marketing managers are usually stressful, particularly near deadlines. They may travel to meet with clients or representatives of communications media.

ANNOUNCERS

SIGNIFICANT POINTS

- Most announcers work full-time, some part-time.

- On-air shifts may vary.

NATURE OF THE WORK

Announcers present news and sports and may provide commentary or interview guests about these topics or other important events.

TRAINING

Educational requirements for announcers vary. Radio and television announcers typically have a bachelor's degree in journalism, broadcasting, or communications, along with work experience at their college radio or television station. Public address announcers typically need a high school diploma, along with short-term on-the-job training.

OTHER QUALIFICATIONS

Work at a radio or TV station while in college is helpful in obtaining a first job. Qualities include appearance, computer skills, people skills, persistence, research skills, and speaking and writing skills.

ADVANCEMENT

Most announcers work a few years in a small broadcasting market to obtain experience and develop followings.

JOB OUTLOOK

Employment of radio and television announcers is projected to grow by 7 percent from 2010 to 2020, slower than the average for all occupations. Employment of public address system and other announcers is projected to grow by 5 percent from 2010 to 2020, slower than the average for all occupations. Experienced, formally trained announcers should have the best job prospects.

WORK ENVIRONMENT

Many announcers work in radio and television studios. Others work for sports teams or are self-employed. Many announcers work part-time.

ART DIRECTORS AND GRAPHIC DESIGNERS

SIGNIFICANT POINTS

- Art directors establish the overall design style for visual projects.

- Graphic designers create the projects.

- They work with clients, design staffs, PR professionals, and others.

- Directors may be responsible for project budgets and timelines.

NATURE OF THE WORK

Art directors are responsible for the visual style and images in magazines, newspapers, product packaging, and movie and television productions. They create the overall design. Graphic designers develop artwork and layouts, creating projects by hand and computer.

TRAINING

Art directors need at least a bachelor's degree in an art or design subject. Graphic designers have degrees in graphic design or a related major.

OTHER QUALIFICATIONS

Depending on the industry, directors may have worked as graphic designers, illustrators, copy editors, or photographers, or in another art or design occupation, before becoming art directors. Qualities of directors include creativity, communication skills, leadership skills, and time-management skills. Qualities of designers are artistic ability, creativity, communication and computer skills, time-management skills, and teamwork skills.

ADVANCEMENT

For many artists, including art directors, developing a portfolio—a collection of an artist's work that demonstrates his or her styles and abilities—is essential. Graphic designers usually work one to three years before advancing to senior positions.

OUTLOOK

Employment of art directors is expected to increase 9 percent from 2010 to 2020. For graphic designers, it should increase 13 percent. Art directors will continue to be needed to oversee the work of graphic designers, illustrators, photographers, and others who design in artwork or layouts. For designers, competition will be strong, especially for senior graphic design positions. Web design experience will be a great asset.

WORK ENVIRONMENT

Art directors and designers work for advertising and public relations firms, newspaper and magazine publishers, specialized design services firms, and the motion picture and video industries. Designers work with computer and hand tools in studios.

BROADCAST AND SOUND ENGINEERING TECHNICIANS

SIGNIFICANT POINTS

- Technicians generally work full-time.

- Weekend work may be required, depending on the radio or TV station's programming schedule.

NATURE OF THE WORK

Broadcast and sound engineering technicians set up, operate, and maintain the electrical equipment for radio and television broadcasts and other broadcast productions.

TRAINING

Most broadcast and sound engineering technicians have an associate's degree or vocational certification, although some are hired with only a high school diploma. Some formal training, gained through either work experience or education, is often required.

OTHER QUALIFICATIONS

Technicians need computer skills, manual dexterity, communication skills, technical skills, and problem-solving skills.

ADVANCEMENT

Although many broadcast and sound engineering technicians work first in small markets or with small stations in big markets, after they gain the necessary experience and skills, they often transfer to larger, better-paying radio or television stations. Large stations almost never hire someone without previous experience, and they value more specialized skills. Experienced workers with strong technical skills can become supervisory technicians or chief engineers. A college degree in engineering is typically needed to become chief engineer at large television stations.

JOB OUTLOOK

Employment of broadcast and sound engineering technicians is expected to grow 10 percent from 2010 to 2020, about as fast as the average for all occupations. Growth is expected as businesses, schools, and radio and television stations demand new equipment to improve their audio and video capabilities.

WORK ENVIRONMENT

Broadcast and sound engineering technicians generally work indoors in office buildings and radio, television, or recording studios. However, those who broadcast news and other programs outside the studio may work outdoors in all types of weather. Technicians typically work full-time.

FILM AND VIDEO EDITORS AND CAMERA OPERATORS

SIGNIFICANT POINTS

- In broadcasting, job growth is expected to be slow because automatic camera systems reduce the need for camera operators at many TV stations.

- Production companies are experimenting with new content delivery methods such as mobile and online TV, which may lead to more work for operators in the future.

- Work hours vary. Long hours may be required when on deadline.

NATURE OF THE WORK

Film and video editors and camera operators record images that entertain or inform an audience. Camera operators capture a wide range of material for TV shows, motion pictures, music videos, documentaries, or news and sporting events. Editors construct the final productions from the many different images camera operators capture. They collaborate with producers and directors to create the final production.

TRAINING

Camera operators typically need a bachelor's degree and some on-the-job training. Most film editors have a bachelor's degree and several years of experience as an assistant to a film editor.

OTHER QUALIFICATIONS

These professionals must be creative and detail-oriented. They must have good technical skills, vision, and eye-hand coordination.

ADVANCEMENT

Some camera operators become producers or directors.

JOB OUTLOOK

Employment of film and video editors is projected to grow 5 percent from 2010 to 2020. Employment of camera operators is projected to grow 2 percent. These growth rates are slower than the average rates for all jobs.

WORK ENVIRONMENT

Camera operators and editors work in studios and on location. Some camera operators work in uncomfortable or even dangerous conditions, such as severe weather, military conflicts, and natural disasters. They may have to stand for long periods waiting for an event to take place. They may carry heavy equipment.

MEETING, CONVENTION, AND EVENT PLANNERS

SIGNIFICANT POINTS

- Despite the spread of online communication media, face-to-face interaction is invaluable. For that reason, growth in this job market is expected to grow vigorously.

- Planners regularly collaborate with clients, hospitality workers, and meeting attendees.

NATURE OF THE WORK

Meeting, convention, and event planners coordinate all aspects of professional meetings and events. They choose meeting locations, arrange transportation, and coordinate other details.

TRAINING

Applicants should have at least a bachelor's degree and some related work experience in planning. Job opportunities should be best for those with a bachelor's degree in hospitality management.

OTHER QUALIFICATIONS

Essential qualities for planners include communication skills, composure, computer skills, customer service skills, interpersonal skills, negotiation skills, organizational skills, and problem-solving skills.

ADVANCEMENT

Job opportunities should be best for people with a bachelor's degree in hospitality management. A Certified Meeting Planner (CMP) credential is also viewed favorably by potential employers. Those who have experience with virtual meeting software and social media outlets should also have an advantage in the job search. Planners can expect strong competition for jobs. Those with related work experience should have the best job opportunities.

JOB OUTLOOK

Employment of meeting, convention, and event planners is expected to grow 44 percent from 2010 to 2020, much faster than the average for all occupations. As businesses and organizations become increasingly international, meetings and conventions are expected to become even more important.

WORK ENVIRONMENT

Meeting, convention, and event planners spend most of their time in offices. During meetings and events, they usually work on-site at hotels or convention centers. They travel regularly to attend events they organize and to visit prospective meeting sites.

PHOTOGRAPHERS

SIGNIFICANT POINTS

- Photographers must be familiar with a variety of digital cameras and equipment as well as photo-editing software.

- Many publications hire freelance photographers. Competition among freelancers is particularly stiff.

NATURE OF THE WORK

Photographers use their technical expertise, creativity, and composition skills to produce and preserve images that visually tell a story or record an event.

TRAINING

Postsecondary education is not required for some photography work. Photojournalists often need a bachelor's degree.

OTHER QUALIFICATIONS

Photographers need artistic ability, computer skills, detail-oriented skills, and interpersonal skills. Business and customer service skills are important for self-employed photographers.

ADVANCEMENT

Job prospects will be best for candidates who are multi-talented and possess related skills such as picture editing and capturing digital video.

JOB OUTLOOK

Employment of photographers is projected to grow by 13 percent from 2010 to 2020, about as fast as the average for all occupations. Overall growth will be limited because of the decreasing cost of digital cameras and the increasing number of amateur photographers and hobbyists.

Employment of self-employed photographers is expected to grow by 15 percent from 2010 to 2020.

WORK ENVIRONMENT

News and sports photographers may travel locally or long-distance. News photographers often work long, irregular hours in uncomfortable or even dangerous surroundings and must be available to work on short notice. Most photographers stand or walk for long periods while carrying heavy equipment.

PRODUCERS AND DIRECTORS

SIGNIFICANT POINTS

- Producers and directors frequently work under pressure.

- They ensure that each production is executed satisfactorily and on schedule.

NATURE OF THE WORK

Producers and directors are in charge of creating broadcast, film, and other types of productions. Producers have overall responsibility for the production. Directors oversee the work of each member of the broadcast team.

TRAINING

There are few formal training programs. Most producers and directors for television and radio presentations have degrees in broadcasting or other communications curricula.

OTHER QUALIFICATIONS

Producers and directors need communication, leadership, and management skills as well as creativity.

ADVANCEMENT

Producers and directors may be given better jobs and more complex projects as their experience increases and reputations grow.

JOB OUTLOOK

Employment of producers and directors is projected to grow 11 percent from 2010 to 2020, about as fast as the average for all occupations.

WORK ENVIRONMENT

Work hours for producers and directors of sports programs and broadcasts may be long and irregular. Evening, weekend, and holiday work is common.

PUBLIC RELATIONS MANAGERS AND SPECIALISTS

SIGNIFICANT POINTS

- If a client becomes the subject of unfavorable publicity, public relations specialists are expected to respond to news developments and maintain their organization's reputation.

- Increasingly, public relations work involves social media and other online platforms.

NATURE OF THE WORK

Public relations managers and specialists create and maintain a favorable public image for their employer or client. They write material for media releases, plan and direct public relations programs, and raise funds for their organizations.

TRAINING

A bachelor's degree is typically needed for public relations manager and specialist positions. Public relations managers must also have related work experience.

OTHER QUALIFICATIONS

Public relations personnel must have interpersonal, organizational, problem-solving, and research skills. They must be good writers and speakers.

ADVANCEMENT

With the increased use of social media for public relations, professionals experienced in social media platforms have an advantage.

JOB OUTLOOK

Employment of public relations managers and specialists is expected to grow 21 percent from 2010 to 2020, faster than the average for all occupations.

WORK ENVIRONMENT

Public relations managers and specialists usually work in offices, but they also deliver speeches, attend meetings and community activities, and travel. They work in fairly high-stress environments, often managing and organizing several events at the same time.

REPORTERS, CORRESPONDENTS, AND BROADCAST NEWS ANALYSTS

SIGNIFICANT POINTS

- Internships and experience working for school newspapers and broadcast stations is valuable for entering the job market.

- First job opportunities are better at small newspapers and broadcast stations. Competition is especially strong in large media markets.

NATURE OF THE WORK

Reporters, correspondents, and broadcast news analysts inform the public about news and events happening internationally, nationally, and locally. They report the news for newspapers, magazines, Web sites, television, and radio.

TRAINING

Most employers prefer workers who have a bachelor's degree in journalism or communications. However, some employers hire applicants who have a degree in a related subject such as English or political science if they have relevant work experience.

OTHER QUALIFICATIONS

Reporters, journalists, and news analysts need good objectivity, communication skills, people skills, persistence, and stamina.

ADVANCEMENT

With experience, reporters and correspondents can advance from news organizations in small cities or towns to news organizations in large cities. Alternatively, they may become editors or news directors.

JOB OUTLOOK

Employment of reporters and correspondents is expected to steadily decline by 8 percent from 2010 to 2020. Declines are expected because of the consolidation of news organizations, decreases in the readership of newspapers, and declines in viewership for many news television shows.

Employment of broadcast news analysts is expected to grow by 10 percent from 2010 to 2020, about as fast as the average for all occupations. Growth is expected as news agencies prefer news analysts over traditional reporters to provide insight and commentary about the news.

WORK ENVIRONMENT

Reporters, correspondents, and broadcast news analysts spend a lot of time in the field conducting interviews and investigating stories. Many reporters spend little to no time in an office. They travel to be on location for events or to meet contacts and file stories remotely.

Most reporters, correspondents, and broadcast news analysts work full-time. The work of journalists is often fast-paced, with constant demands to meet deadlines and be the first reporter to publish a news story on a subject. When news is breaking, reporters may need to work long hours or change their work schedules to follow the story. Journalists may need to work nights and weekends.

STATISTICIANS

SIGNIFICANT POINTS

- Sports statisticians collect and analyze large amounts of data. Some statisticians design surveys, experiments, and opinion polls to collect information.

- Statisticians often work in teams with other professionals.

NATURE OF THE WORK

Statisticians use mathematical techniques to analyze and interpret data and draw conclusions.

TRAINING

Most statisticians enter the occupation with a master's degree in statistics, mathematics, or survey methodology, although a bachelor's degree is sufficient for some entry-level jobs. Research and academic jobs generally require a Ph.D.

OTHER QUALIFICATIONS

Statisticians need exceptional critical thinking, problem-solving, writing, and speaking skills.

ADVANCEMENT

Opportunities for promotion are greater for individuals with a master's degree or Ph.D. Statisticians with a master's degree or Ph.D. usually can design their own work. They may develop new statistical methods and become independent consultants.

JOB OUTLOOK

Employment of statisticians is expected to increase by 14 percent from 2010 to 2020, as fast as the average for all occupations.

WORK ENVIRONMENT

Although statisticians work mostly in offices, they may travel in order to supervise surveys or gather data. Sometimes they must work overtime to meet deadlines.

WRITERS, AUTHORS, AND EDITORS

SIGNIFICANT POINTS

- Because of deadlines, work can be stressful and tiring.

- Schedules may be flexible.

- Freelance writers usually work on assignment.

NATURE OF THE WORK

Writers and authors develop original written content for advertisements, books, magazines, movie and television scripts, and online publications. Editors plan, review, and revise content for publication. Many editors are employed by newspapers.

TRAINING

A college degree generally is required for a salaried position as a writer, author, or editor. Typical majors are journalism, communications, and English. Proficiency with computers, graphic design, and multimedia software is recommended; communications equipment skills may be necessary to stay in touch with sources and one another while working on assignments. Excellent writing skills are essential.

OTHER QUALIFICATIONS

Necessary writer qualities include creativity, determination, persuasion, and social perceptiveness—in addition to writing and language skills. Editors also need decision-making and interpersonal skills for working with writers. They must be detail-oriented.

ADVANCEMENT

Writers and authors generally advance by building a reputation, taking on more complex writing assignments, and getting published in more prestigious markets and publications. Having previously published work that was well received and maintaining a track record of meeting deadlines are important for advancement. Writing for smaller businesses, local newspapers, advertising agencies, and not-for-profit organizations allows beginning writers and authors to start taking credit for their work immediately. However, opportunities for advancement within these organizations may be limited because they either do not have enough regular work or do not need more advanced writing.

Most editors begin work as writers. Those who are particularly skilled at identifying stories, correcting writing style, and interacting with writers may be interested in editing jobs.

JOB OUTLOOK

Employment of writers and authors is projected to grow 6 percent from 2010 to 2020, slower than the average for all occupations. Strong competition is expected for salaried writing jobs because many people are attracted to this occupation.

Employment of editors is expected to experience little or no change from 2010 to 2020 as print media continue to face strong pressure from online publications. Strong competition is expected for salaried editing jobs because many people want to work in the media industry.

WORK ENVIRONMENT

Writers and authors work in an office, at home, or wherever they have access to a computer. Most writers and authors work full-time. However, self-employed and freelance writers usually work part-time or have variable schedules.

Editors usually work in offices, but advances in technology now allow some editors to work wherever they have a computer.

GLOSSARY

ad revenue Income earned through advertising sales.

bossaball New sport similar to volleyball but played on an inflated, bouncy surface.

brand An organization's familiar identifier, such as its logo, nickname, or mascot.

byline Reporter's name appearing at the top of a printed or online article.

color commentary Explanations and insights provided by an expert, typically a former athlete, during sports broadcasts.

disk golf Sport similar to golf in which players circuit a course aiming a flying disk at posted baskets.

freelance Self-employed, accepting work assignments for multiple publications.

good copy A well-written draft article submitted by a reporter to an editor.

help desk Information station, phone extension, or Web site Q&A section.

Internet radio Online audio service that presents listeners with streaming media files; also Web radio or e-radio.

masthead Section near the front of a print publication listing the staff, contact information, and other publisher details.

netcast Broadcast of an event via the Internet.

panning Photographic technique that gives the subject of a still photo the appearance of moving against a blurred background.

periodical A medium—newspaper, magazine, or newsletter—published at regular intervals.

perseverance Determination in doing something despite difficulty or delay in achieving success.

pitch To offer a publicity story to media editors.

podcast A digital video or audio recording made available to Internet users.

portfolio Selection of work an artist or photographer uses for marketing.

press kit Packet of informational and promotional materials about a client firm, prepared for reporters by the client's PR department.

scoop First publication of breaking news, beating rival publications.

stock photos A photographer or photo service's inventory of photographs, each of them available to multiple buyers.

streaming media Timely Internet content sent to subscribers as it becomes available.

stringer Freelancer for a newspaper who covers a specific topic, such as a high school's sports, not covered by the newspaper staff.

strip photography Capturing a rapid sequence of still images to follow action step by step.

syndication Simultaneous distribution of a news story or broadcast to multiple newspapers or broadcast stations.

virtual meeting Live conference in which the participants are in different locations, connected by computer and/or phone.

whitepaper In-depth report presenting an organization's mission, organizational structure, research findings, etc.

wire service News syndicate.

FOR MORE INFORMATION

Art Directors Guild (ADG)
11969 Ventura Boulevard, 2nd Floor
Studio City, CA 91604
(818) 762-9995
Web site: http://www.adg.org
The guild is comprised of art directors, graphic artists, illustrators, scenic artists, set designers, and other art professionals.

Association for Women in Sports Media (AWSM)
7742 Spalding Drive, #377
Norcross, GA 30092
Web site: http://www.awsmonline.org
The advocacy group supports female sportswriters and editors, as well as professionals in broadcast production and public/media relations.

Canadian Association for Photographic Art (CAPA)
Box 357
Logan Lake, BC V0K 1W0
Canada
Web site: http://capacanada.ca
The association promotes "the art and science of photography in all its forms throughout Canada and the world" and seeks to promote public interest in photography.

Canadian Public Relations Society (CPRS)
Suite 346, 4195 Dundas Street West
Toronto, ON M8X 1Y4

Canada

(416) 239-7034

Web site: http://www.cprs.ca

Members "work to maintain the highest standards and to share a uniquely Canadian experience in public relations."

International Sports Press Association (AIPS)

Avenue de Rhodani 54

1007 Lausanne, Switzerland

Web site: http://www.aipsmedia.com

The association unites more than 140 press organizations worldwide in promoting sports journalists' interests and education.

National Association of Broadcasters (NAB)

771 N Street NW

Washington, DC 20036

(202) 429-5300

Web site: http://www.nab.org

This trade association strives to serve as "the voice for the nation's radio and television broadcasters."

Public Relations Society of America (PRSA)

33 Maiden Lane, 11th Floor

New York, NY 10038-5150

(212) 460-1400

Web site: http://www.prsa.org

The PRSA provides professional development, sets standards of excellence, and upholds ethical principles for public relations workers.

Society of Broadcast Engineers (SBE)

9102 N. Meridian Street, Suite 150

Indianapolis, IN 46260

(317) 846-9000

Web site: http://www.sbe.org

The SBE is devoted to advancing all levels and categories of
broadcast engineering.

Sports Journalists' Association

Unit 92, Capital Business Centre

22 Carlton Road

Surrey, England CR2 0BS

United Kingdom

Web site: http://www.sportsjournalists.co.uk

Based in the United Kingdon, this international body keeps
up with changes in the profession and provides various
member activities and resources.

Sports Photographers Association of America (SPAA)

2282 Springport Road, Suite F

Jackson, MI 49202

(800) 762-9287, (517) 788-8100

Web site: http://www.pmai.org/spaa

The SPAA is part of the Worldwide Community of Imaging
Associations (PMA). It offers educational programs,
networking, events, and research and business services
for sports photographers.

WEB SITES

Due to the changing nature of Internet links, Rosen Publishing
has developed an online list of Web sites related to the subject of
this book. This site is updated regularly. Please use this link to
access the list:

http://www.rosenlinks.com/GCSI/Media

FOR FURTHER READING

Biskup, Agnieszka. *Football: How It Works* (The Science of Sports). Mankato, ME: Capstone Press, 2010.

Field, Shelley. *Career Opportunities in the Sports Industry*. New York, NY: Checkmark Books, 2010.

Greenwald, John. *Field Guides to Finding a New Career: Sports Industry*. New York, NY: Ferguson Publishing, 2010.

Harmon, Daniel E. *Careers as a Marketing and Public Relations Specialist* (Essential Careers). New York, NY: Rosen Publishing, 2014.

Harmon, Daniel E. *First Job Smarts* (Get $mart with Your Money). New York, NY: Rosen Publishing, 2010.

Howell, Brian. *Sports* (Inside the Industry). San Francisco, CA: Essential Library, 2011.

Lambert, Stephen. *Great Jobs for Business Majors* (Great Jobs for . . . Majors). New York, NY: McGraw-Hill, 2008.

Macy, Sue. *Swifter, Higher, Stronger: A Photographic History of the Summer Olympics*. Des Moines, IA: National Geographic Children's Books, 2008.

McLeish, Ewan. *Sports Industry* (A Closer Look: Global Industries). New York, NY: Rosen Publishing, 2011.

Moore, Edward. *School Public Relations for Student Success*. Thousand Oaks, CA: Corwin, 2009.

Public Relations (Ferguson's Careers in Focus). New York, NY: Ferguson Publishing, 2007.

Reeves, Diana Lindsey. *Career Ideas for Kids Who Like Sports*. 2nd ed. New York, NY: Checkmark Books, 2007.

Salter, Brian. *Successful Public Relations in a Week* (Teach Yourself: Business). New York, NY: McGraw-Hill, 2013.

Sports (Discovering Careers). New York, NY: Facts On File, Inc., 2010.

Sports Illustrated. The Basketball Book by Editors of Sports *Illustrated*. New York, NY: Sports Illustrated, 2007.

Tymorek, Stan. *Advertising and Public Relations* (Career Launcher). New York, NY: Checkmark Books, 2010.

Wells, Michelle, Andy Kreutzer, and Jim Kahler. *A Career in Sports: Advice from Sports Business Leaders*. Livonia, MI: M. Wells Enterprises, 2010.

What Can I Do Now? Exploring Careers for Your Future. 2nd ed. New York, NY: Ferguson Publishing, 2007.

Wong, Glenn M. *The Comprehensive Guide to Careers in Sports*. Sudbury, MA: Jones & Bartlett, 2008.

Bercovici, Jeff. "Despite Digital Gains, Newspaper Circulation Backslides." *Forbes*, April 30, 2013. Retrieved July 2013 (http://www.forbes.com/sites/jeffbercovici/2013/04/30/despite-digital-gains-newspaper-circulation-backslides).

Edmonds, Rick, et al. "Newspapers: Building Digital Revenues Proves Painfully Slow." Pew Research Center's Project for Excellence in Journalism, "The State of the News Media 2012." February 11, 2013. Retrieved July 2013 (http://stateofthemedia.org/2012/newspapers-building-digital-revenues-proves-painfully-slow).

ESPN MediaZone "Holly Rowe: Commentator." Retrieved August 2013 (http://espnmediazone.com/us/bios/rowe_holly).

ESPN MediaZone "Lisa Salters: Commentator." Retrieved August 2013 (http://espnmediazone.com/us/bios/salters_lisa).

Fountain, Charles. *Sportswriter: The Life and Times of Grantland Rice*. New York, NY: Oxford University Press, Inc., 1993.

Katzowitz, Josh. "The Anatomy of a Deadline Story." *Josh Katzowitz—Sports Writer/Author Thinker* blog. February 8, 2010. Retrieved September 2013 (http://joshkatzowitz.com/2010/02/08/the-anatomy-of-a-deadline-story).

Kindred, Dave. "A Deadline Column About Writing on Deadline." National Sports Journalism Center, *Our Voices* blog. January 28, 2010. Retrieved September 2013 (http://sportsjournalism.org/sports-media-news/a-deadline-column-about-writing-on-deadline).

Pumerantz, Zack. "20 Crazy Sports Stats You Never Knew." BleacherReport.com, June 20, 2012. Retrieved August

2013 (http://bleacherreport.com/articles/1227516-20-crazy-sports-stats-you-never-knew).

Rice, Grantland. *Only the Brave and Other Poems*. New York, NY: A. S. Barnes and Company, 1941.

Smith, Mari. "12 Tenets of Relationship Marketing Effectiveness." MariSmith.com, October 27, 2011. Retrieved April 2013 (http://www.marismith.com/tenets-of-relationship-marketing-effectiveness).

Stewart, Megan. "Griner, Rowe Show Crucial Player-Reporter Relationship." *AWSM*, July 8, 2013. Retrieved August 2013 (http://awsmonline.org/wnbas-brittney-griner-and-espns-holly-rowe-demonstrate-crucial-relationship/#more-3188).

Talty, John. "Top 50 Sports Writers to Follow on Twitter." *International Business Times*, March 27, 2012. Retrieved August 2013 (http://www.ibtimes.com/top-50-sports-writers-follow-twitter-430734).

Thomas, Katie. "ESPN Slowly Introducing Online Brand for Women." *New York Times*, October 15, 2010. Retrieved August 2013 (http://www.nytimes.com/2010/10/16/sports/16espnw.html?_r=0).

"Title IX Is Mine: Holly Rowe." From "The Power of IX," espnW, April 27, 2012. Retrieved August 2013 (http://espn.go.com/video/clip?id=7863288).

U.S. Department of Labor. Bureau of Labor Statistics. *Occupation Outlook Handbook*. Retrieved August, September 2013 (http://www.bls.gov/ooh).

INDEX

ABOUT THE AUTHOR

Daniel E. Harmon is a former newspaper sports reporter, columnist, editor, and award-winning sports photographer. He once almost died chasing an opposing back while researching an article on rugby. He is the author of more than eighty books and thousands of magazine and newspaper articles. His previous books on sports topics include *Grappling and Submission Grappling* and *Notre Dame Football*.

PHOTO CREDITS

Cover, p. 1 (sports commentator) © iStockphoto.com/Steve Debenport; cover, p. 1 (field) © iStockphoto.com/herreid; pp. 4–5, 21, 23, 46, 54, 62, 72, 74–75, 89, 91 © AP Images; pp. 9, 104 Copyright 2013 NBAE. Photo by Jesse D. Garrabrant/NBAE/Getty Images; p. 12 Justin Jay/Getty Images; p. 17 antb/Shutterstock.com; p. 19 Scott J. Ferrell/CQ-Roll Call Group/Getty Images; p. 32 Porter Binks/Sports Illustrated/Getty Images; p. 34 wavebreakmedia/Shutterstock.com; pp. 42–43, 77 (bottom) Bloomberg/Getty Images; p. 45 Gabriel Bouys/AFP/Getty Images; p. 50 Mandel Ngan/AFP/Getty Images; pp. 60–61 Steve Debenport/E+/Getty Images; pp. 66–67 Mike Zarrilli/Getty Images; p. 69 Darren Carroll/Getty Images; p. 82 © Brian Westerholt/Sports on Film; p. 84 Copyright 2012 NBAE. Photo by Andrew D. Bernstein/NBAE/Getty Images; p. 94 Paulo Whitaker/Reuters/Landov; p. 97 laflor/Vetta/Getty Images; p. 107 AFP/Getty Images; interior design elements (graph) © iStockphoto.com/ hudiemm, (stripes) Lost & Taken; pp. 8, 20, 29, 44, 58, 77 (top), 87, 102, 109, 112, 123, 147, 149, 152, 154, 156 © iStockphoto.com unless otherwise noted. From top left ultramarinfoto, Kayann, VIPDesignUSA, plherrera, cb34inc, yai112, Jimmy Anderson, dbrskinner, dswebb, Gannet77, Sergieiev/ Shutterstock.com, gzaleckas, choja, cscredon, peepo.

Designer: Brian Garvey; Editor: Kathy Kuhtz Campbell; Photo Researcher: Marty Levick